THE ABC's of Classroom Management

Second Edition

**An A–Z sampler
for designing your
learning community**

The ABC's of Classroom Management

Second Edition

An A–Z sampler for designing your learning community

by Pamela A. Kramer Ertel
and Madeline Kovarik

KAPPA DELTA PI
INTERNATIONAL HONOR SOCIETY IN EDUCATION

Routledge
Taylor & Francis Group

NEW YORK AND LONDON

This edition published 2014
by Routledge
711 Third Avenue, New York, NY 10017

Simultaneously published in the UK
by Routledge
2 Park Square, Milton Park, Abingdon, Oxon OX14 4RN

*Routledge is an imprint of the Taylor & Francis Group,
an informa business*

First edition published 2005 by Kappa Delta Pi

Library of Congress Cataloging-in-Publication Data

Ertel, Pamela A Kramer, 1956–
   The ABC's of classroom management : an A-Z sampler for designing your learning community / by Pamela A. Kramer Ertel and Madeline Kovarik, Kappa Delta Pi. — Second edition.
       pages cm
Includes bibliographical references and index.
   1. Classroom management—Handbooks, manuals, etc.   I. Kappa Delta Pi (Honor society)   II. Title.
   LB3013.K73   2013
   371.102'4—dc23
   2013004946

ISBN: 978-0-415-84171-9 (pbk)
ISBN: 978-0-203-76533-3 (ebk)

Typeset in Times New Roman PS
by Apex CoVantage

SUSTAINABLE FORESTRY INITIATIVE
Certified Sourcing
www.sfiprogram.org
SFI-00555
The SFI label applies to the text stock.

Printed and bound in the United States of America by Walsworth Publishing Company, Marceline, MO.

Table of Contents

Contents

Contents

References **149**

Extras

Dedication

I dedicate this book to my parents, Hank and Angela Gialanella, who taught me the meaning of unconditional love. Unconditional love is a crucial characteristic of an effective educator.

Special thanks to Sister Claire Whalen, formerly of Marian College, Indianapolis. You are an outstanding model of an effective teacher educator and a lifelong learner, and you have provided a lifetime of inspiration to me.

—Pamela Kramer Ertel

Contributors

Executive Director
Faye Snodgress

Director of Publications
Kathie-Jo Arnoff

Series Editor
Karen L. Allen

Assistant Editor
Laurie Quay

Design
Chuck Jarrell

Cartoonist
Bill Allen

Reviewers
Eric Combs
Nichole Wangsgard
Michael Putman
Rebekah Stathakis

Contributors
Sarah Wolfe Hartman
Marge James
Erika Lee
Maegan McCord
Andrea Sabatini McLoughlin
Theresa Knipstein Meyer
Amy Dyer Moore
Nichole Wangsgard

About the Authors

Pamela A. Kramer Ertel is Dean of the College of Education at East Stroudsburg University of Pennsylvania, where she served as a Professor in the Department of Early Childhood and Elementary Education prior to becoming Dean. Her array of experience during her 30-plus years in education includes 9 years as an elementary teacher and 18 years as a professor focused on teaching science methods in a Professional Development School program. Dr. Kramer Ertel's research interests include classroom management and integrating literature in various content areas. She also is a longtime Counselor of Kappa Delta Pi's Gamma Xi Chapter at ESU. Even as an administrator, Dr. Ertel continues to seek opportunities to teach children, one of them as a third- and fourth-grade Sunday School Teacher at her church. "It keeps me real," she said.

Madeline Kovarik has served in the field of education for more than 30 years as an assistant professor, elementary teacher, guidance counselor, primary specialist, and school administrator. Throughout her career, she has focused on the practical application of educational theory and instructional skills that help both students and teachers succeed in the classroom. Always keeping the teacher experience in mind and focused on finding meaningful ways to help educators succeed, Dr. Kovarik writes journal articles, speaks at local, state, and international conferences, and volunteers for educational organizations. Her guiding philosophy is "Good teachers help create good students who, in turn, will create a good future for all of society."

About *The ABC's of Classroom Management*

Effective classroom management is one of the most essential skill sets administrators seek when hiring new teachers, because a well-managed classroom is central to a successful and safe learning environment. As crucial as this skill set is, classroom management is an area in which many new teachers are not thoroughly prepared or confident once in the classroom. Furthermore, managing a classroom is an ongoing process that even experienced educators can find challenging.

Take heart, though. *The ABC's of Classroom Management*, 2nd edition, provides the foundations of classroom management with evidenced-based information and practical applications to start you out on the right foot. It explains fundamental procedures and organizational techniques, as well as operational concepts and applications for building on that foundation, with topics covering both current classroom challenges and issues that have plagued educators for years.

The ABC's of Classroom Management, 2nd edition, offers more than 100 new topics, along with expanded versions of long-standing topics from the 1st edition, such as behavior management, communication, discipline, and procedures. New entries include such timely topics and examples in the classroom as accountability, cyberbullying, friending students, reality check, social media, and violence prevention. Illustrated examples, ideas, cartoons, and more than 40 real-life tips and advice augment the book's content and are designated by the following icons.

Watch for the exclamation icons for quick tips that have been tested and tried by experienced educators.

You'll find words of wisdom and real-life examples at the sign of the apple.

---

66 99 Look for more words of wisdom, as well as inspiration or humor when you come across this graphic.

A bonus to the 2nd edition of *The ABC's of Classroom Management* and Kappa Delta Pi's ABC book series is the addition of a resource website. At *ABC's Online*, www.kdp.org/teachingresources/ABConline.php, you can access additional information on many ABC topics, download related forms and instructions, find classroom tools, and link to other resource sites.

As in the 1st edition, the well-organized alphabetical format allows you to quickly locate the issue challenging you at the moment, check suggested related topics (boldfaced), and form a plan that best fits you and your students. New and future teachers can appreciate the ease of using *The ABC's of Classroom Management* to gain management tips and tools they can apply right away. Simplicity and practicality, however, are not the only benefits of this book and companion website. Underlying the nuts-and-bolts entries are the themes of teacher professionalism, leadership, and empowerment. Armed with a proactive attitude and the right tools, applied purposefully and consistently, novice teachers develop their craft to become effective classroom managers and masterful educators.

Absent Students

Creating a plan for the inevitable student absences before they occur gets you ready and keeps students from missing a beat when they return to class. Have a set of absent folders in a predetermined location where returning students retrieve the homework and paperwork they missed. Or enlist classmates to help by placing the information in the folder or on the desk of an absent student while distributing assignments, worksheets, or notes. If age appropriate, you may ask a student to take notes and explain directions to the absent child to help keep him or her current. If you change classes during the day, have a file folder for each class period.

Accountability for Students

Holding students accountable for their behavior is critical to a well-managed classroom. The challenge is determining the appropriate manner for addressing a problem. According to Ryan (2008), students respond much more effectively to private reprimands rather than call-outs of their misbehavior. Addressing only the misbehaving student also avoids distracting others from their work. Furthermore, private discussions minimize repeat misbehaviors from students who seek attention in negative ways and may be amused at being called out by the teacher.

To increase students' accountability for their actions and participation in appropriate classroom conduct, encourage them to articulate the behaviors that need to be corrected. For example, you might address a student about his wandering eyes during spelling tests: "Noah, what are the classroom rules about taking tests?" After he goes over the rules, he also can talk about how he can help himself concentrate on his own test. A privacy screen, increased studying, or alternative methods of study are among the methods he could mention.

Activity Periods and Specials

No matter how well students behave in your classroom, they may take advantage of situations away from the room, such as during art, music, PE, or lunch. If the professional in charge leaves handling the behavior to the classroom teacher, consequences for the student's actions are delayed, a less than ideal situation. Without recency—a connection between the time the misbehavior occurs and its consequence—students are less likely to connect the action and resulting consequence and more likely to repeat the behavior.

Again, prevention is the best remedy. Conduct a class meeting specifically to discuss behavior outside the classroom with the focus on how class rules apply in all situations. The discussion must delineate the consequence for future misbehaviors. If an incident already has occurred, be sure to avoid a "He did this …" or tattletale session. Consequences must be applied consistently. Behavior contracts (see **Contracts**), developed and signed by all classroom members, effectively address behavior outside the classroom.

Anger Management

When a student seems to have anger management issues, it is best to focus on preventing outbursts. Some students get very angry when they become frustrated with a task or situation. Monitoring these students is crucial to intervention and curbing out-of-control anger. With appropriate levels of support for the student, you can reduce his or her frustrations and, therefore, ward off an explosive reaction. Supportive actions include helping the student break down the project into small steps or giving periodic breaks from difficult tasks to keep the student calm. When a student does have an angry outburst, he or she needs to move to a designated area in your classroom or school to ensure the safety of everyone. In cases of severe anger, seek assistance from others, such as the school counselor, your administrator, and the parents. You may need to seek a referral for external personal or family counseling.

What if you have anger management issues or find yourself very frustrated in certain classroom situations? You need a plan for addressing situations that set you off. If a noisy classroom frazzles your last nerve, you must have a method that stops noise escalation before it gets to that nerve. For best practices, develop several strategies for preventing angry outbursts. Though it may sound trite, taking a deep breath and counting to 10 before responding to a situation does help. See **Keeping Your Cool** for more suggestions.

Antecedents

Antecedents are events that occur prior to a classroom disruption: the potential triggers to misbehaviors. Have you noticed, for example, that Brantley tends to have a temper tantrum or mood change following lunch or activity period? Does

Jenna's behavior spiral downward when she sits by the window? Looking for patterns and triggers helps teachers understand the function of the behavior and is the first step in managing student behavior. Recording exactly when a student acts out and what occurred immediately prior in a log similar to the one shown here helps determine antecedents. A pattern may not always exist, but looking for antecedents is an excellent beginning behavior analysis (see also **Behavior Analysis** and **Behavior Log**).

Antecedents

Date	Time	Behavior	Antecedent

Assignment avoidance actions

Sometimes my students look purposeful, but they are really avoiding their assignment. When I see one girl get a tissue, put on hand sanitizer, or retrieve an item from her book box, I know she is trying to escape work. Even after encouragement to return to her seat, she waits until she thinks I am engaged with other students and gets up again. When that happens, I check to see that the student understands the work and has the skills needed, and I offer a chance to earn a reward for successfully finished assignments.

> —Nichole Wangsgard, Assistant Professor of Special Education, Southern Utah University, and former Junior High Special Education Teacher

Anticipate

Anticipate anything. Anticipating potential questions, interruptions, and problems helps you prepare for and lessen unexpected incidents. After all, "an ounce of prevention is worth a pound of cure." A wise teacher considers and anticipates problems and challenges that could surface in the course of a lesson or activity. Anticipating is not limited to what might go wrong. It also considers questions or misunderstandings students might have. Thinking in advance helps prevent, lessen, or eliminate potential problems. For example, one teacher anticipated the

Anticipate and Act

Anticipated Challenge	Contingency Plan
What if a student forgets to bring in materials requested for the special craft project?	a. Have additional supplies on hand. b. Prepare an alternate activity with materials available. This craft then also includes a lesson in responsibility.
You are eager for students to participate in amazing Web Quest activities. What if the Internet goes down or you can't access the sites?	a. Plan an offline interactive activity. b. Brainstorm a possible Web Quest of your own.
Students are restless, so you want to have an outdoor science lesson collecting rock samples. What if it rains?	a. Develop your own sample rock collection for students to "discover" indoors. b. Make a "rain date" and review instead. c. "Mine" for rocks in books or on the Web.
Monday is the much-anticipated field trip to the nearby children's museum. What if the bus gets delayed in traffic?	Use the delay time on the bus to rearrange the day's schedule, shortening parts of the trip to make the most of the time left. Flexibility is your friend! P.S. Have students play a guessing game or trivia contest while you rearrange the day.
Your planned and practiced, *awesome* science demonstration flops. Now what?	Turn this seeming "failure" into a teachable moment. Ask students what they expected to happen in the demonstration. Have them determine causes for what might have gone wrong.
At recess your students were engaged in an emotionally heated soccer game. How do you handle tempers and get them settled?	Set the mood for students' return to the classroom. Dim the lights. Play soft, calming music in the background, and select a quiet activity they must begin following recess. In this instance, be sure to respond serenely to the post-game friction.

often asked question "May I get a drink of water?" and allowed students to keep water bottles on their desks. Also see **Assume Nothing**.

Assume Nothing

False assumptions lead to snags in classroom management. They presume that students will understand intent because it is evident to the teacher. Don't take for granted, for example, that telling students to use "inside voices" will result in near-whisper conversations. What if yelling is the norm at their household?

Watch what you assume. Assumptions and vague expectations weave loopholes in any classroom management plan. Get classroom management off to a great start by specifically spelling out your expectations from the first day. Set routines, procedures, and rules, having students help if appropriate, and posting them in the classroom. Remember "five" as the target number of rules for the best following of those rules. Also see **Classroom Management Plan, Routines**, and **Rules**.

Making no assumptions

- Have students repeat your directions to ensure understanding.
- Provide examples of expected behaviors.
- Model expected behaviors.
- Role-play appropriate behavior for and with students.
- Act out proper conduct as well as obviously inappropriate behavior and ask students to reflect on the different scenarios.
- Repeat role-playing scenarios when incidents occur.
- Along with your students, create a chart delineating responsibilities of the teacher and students. Refer to it regularly.
- Remind students of expectations throughout the year.

Attendance

Take attendance and lunch count effortlessly using index and pocket cards—like those once used in library books. With these cards, lunch count and attendance become part of students' morning routine. For each student, select a pocket card and then place the cards in alphabetical order on a board or wall. Below the cards, hang two or three pockets—depending on the school's counting system—for color-coded index cards that signify school lunch, sack lunch, and milk only. A pocket without a card indicates that child is absent. As students arrive and put away their outerwear, they choose the appropriate card, and tuck it into the corresponding name pocket.

For younger children, you can use pictures. Obtain a digital picture of each student and glue it to a magnet. Create a magnetic chart displaying a school at the top, where all magnets are at the beginning of the day, followed by representative pictures underneath: a school lunch, a lunch box, and a lunch box paired with an ice cream or milk. Students move their magnets to the appropriate place. As a class, students count the magnets in each area to complete the lunch form. Unmoved magnets represent absences. Instead of picture magnets, older students can sign in with an "H" for lunch from home or "S" for school lunch.

Attention

Many students misbehave because they want to be noticed by the teacher or other students. In fact, Dreikurs (1968) claimed that 90% of misbehavior is to gain attention.

Among the most obvious attention-seekers are the class clowns. They have learned that acting silly brings them the laughter of classmates and focus from the teacher and they do not care whether the attention received is positive or negative. They want to be noticed whatever way it comes. Even an irritated or disapproving correction from the teacher gives the craved attention.

Remember that attention-seeking is a behavior and behaviors can be modified. The first step in curbing and changing this misbehavior is to ignore minor annoying behaviors while making a point to notice and respond to appropriate behavior. Taking these steps, as shown below, you can facilitate behavior changes in the attention-seeking student. Be patient; behavior change is a slow process occurring over time (also read **Baby Steps**).

Praise good behavior

- Offer verbal praise, such as "You came into the room so quietly today. Your behavior was awesome!"
- Private praise, such as whispering "You are doing a great job of staying quiet today," helps to build confidence.

- A pat on the back while acknowledging an improvement is encouraging: "You are really focused on completing that assignment. Way to go!"

Ignore misbehavior

- Avoid acknowledging behavior when possible or manage it quickly: "You must stop that now. You are disturbing others."

Attention (How Students Get Yours)

Though raising hands is the most common and accepted form for gaining a teacher's attention, other methods can work as well or better. Because students often stop working when they raise their hands, offering alternative methods to signal a need for assistance keeps everyone focused and on task. Try one of the following methods and find related ideas under **Help Desk**.

- **Green/Red Circles.** Cut circles out of green and red paper. Glue the circles together so that one side is green and the other red, laminate, and give one to each student. Students start on green. When they have a question, they flip the circle to red while continuing to work on the task as they can. The teacher scans the room and moves to students who have a red circle.
- **Green/Red Cups.** Cups work well in areas such as a computer lab where it may be difficult to see hands. The red cup sits inside the green cup and rests on the desk or computer top. When assistance is needed, students simply change the order of the cups.

Attention Deficit Hyperactivity Disorder

You may have students who have been diagnosed with Attention Deficit Hyper activity Disorder (ADD/ADHD). Collaborate with the resource teacher to help students with ADHD do well in class. Modifications to the environment, instructional presentation, and assignments, along with a positive, supportive atmosphere can help these students excel in the classroom. Children with ADHD may or may not have other learning difficulties, but most benefit from a structured, yet undemanding environment. They need large tasks broken down into sets of steps to accomplish, along with guidance in transitioning to other subjects or tasks (McIntyre, 2004).

Symptoms range from constant motion and difficulty in focusing on the task at hand to daydreaming or problems in changing tasks. For more resources and detailed information to help your students with ADHD, refer to **Students with Special Needs** in the **Resources** section of this book. Do realize, however, that some students who display these symptoms may be lacking sleep or even have a sleep disorder rather than ADHD. For more information on sleep problems, refer to the alpha entry, **Sleep,** and **Health and safety** in the **Resources** section of **Extras.**

Learning strategies that work

The following strategies are among those recommended by McIntyre (2004), a longtime educator of students with behavior disorders and learning disabilities. Additional strategies are available at www.ldonline.org/article/Strategies_for_Teaching_Youth_with_ADD_and_ADHD.

Interpersonal communication
- Develop good rapport.
- Speak positively and avoid giving commands or student will shut down.

Behavior management
- Ignore many of the negative behaviors and pay special attention to appropriate behavior.
- Provide daily physical activities, such as running errands, erasing the blackboard, doing stretches as a transition.

Modifications
Modifications depend on the individual student and whether additional learning difficulties are involved, but here are a few typical alterations used for students with ADHD:
- Provide a quiet study or test taking area apart from the entire class.
- Allow students to hold a squishy ball, doodle on paper, or bend a pipe cleaner to help them stay on task.

Lessons
- Use more than one modality when giving instructions; also repeat directions.
- Capitalize on students' interests, reference concrete objects when applicable, or use game formats to engage students.

> —Tom McIntyre, Professor of Special Education and
> Coordinator of the Graduate Program in Behavior Disorders,
> Hunter College of the City University of New York

Attention Span

The average attention span of an elementary student varies, but most therapists agree that the best way to calculate attention span is to take the child's age and convert that into minutes (e.g., 7 years old = 7 minutes). If you notice that your class is losing focus or getting restless, then your lesson may be too long for their attention level. Plan the instructional part of your lessons to fit in the expected attention range for the age of your students and preempt possible misbehaviors.

Baby Steps

Behaviors—good or bad—are learned over time. The student who continually calls out may have learned through previous classroom experiences that this response was one way to get the teacher's attention—even if the attention was negative. Just as the behavior developed over time, so will correcting the behavior. Think of this correction as relearning in a series of baby steps. With patience, consistency, and time, you and your student eventually will arrive at the desired destination. Document progress to help both you and the student notice improved behavior (see **Behavior Logs**).

Bathroom Breaks

Student restroom breaks need not interrupt class time or other students. Your school or grade-level team may expect a specific procedure, but if one is not in place, one of these techniques may work for your students.

- **Cards.** Each student has three laminated "restroom break" cards bearing his or her name. To go to the bathroom or drinking fountain, the student places a card in an "I'm in the Restroom" container and then puts the card in a basket upon return. When the cards are used, no more trips are allowed. If another trip is necessary, the student loses a subsequent recess period.
- **Hand signals.** The student holds up one finger and the teacher then nods approval.

- **Index cards.** Index cards bearing each student's name are drawn from a designated box when a restroom break is desired. The student dates or initials the card.
- **Labels.** Computer-generated labels can be stuck in a classroom restroom break book. Once labels are all used, there can be no more breaks until the teacher and student have a meeting.

Be Human

Let students know you as a person. Being "human" is essential to establishing a healthy classroom community. Share information about your family, hobbies, and interests to let students know that you have a life outside of the classroom. Children often think teachers live in their classrooms! Decide what information is reasonable to share. In some areas it may not be safe to make your home location known. In a small community, however, students probably already know where their teachers live. Students should not know intimate details of your life, so take care to maintain a professional distance. Also see **Friending Students**.

Beginning the School Year

When you prepare for the school year and your first teaching position, you are excited about arranging and decorating your classroom, setting up learning centers, and meeting your students. Preparation includes developing curriculum units and planning classroom management; it means determining classroom procedures, rewards, routines, and rules. Being thoroughly prepared also means understanding the culture of your school, even if you do not yet have a class roster.

As soon as you land a position, you can pull all that together, right? The reality is that many new teachers are hired a week or two before school begins. That does not leave much time for all that preparation. Though you may not know when you will be hired, you can build on your teaching philosophy to outline plans for potential positions. You can learn as much as possible about the demographics of the districts to which you apply to gain understanding of the school community and its families. You also can substitute teach to gain awareness of the districts to which you have applied, as well as valuable experience in the profession. Also see **First Day**.

Behavior

Behavior is influenced by many factors. Environment, physical issues, and past experiences all play into a student's and your own actions. Some of these factors can be managed and others are beyond the teacher's control. When developing your strategies for classroom management, remember that no matter how hard you work on them, some behavior issues may require more than you can do. Recognize when you need assistance and know that it is alright to rely on the expertise and advice of peer teachers, former teachers of the student, guidance counselors, and exceptional education personnel. If it "takes a village to raise a child," in education "it takes a professional team of educators to successfully educate a student."

Behavior Analysis

Applied behavior analysis (ABA), once known as behavior modification, looks at the relationship between the specific behavior and the environments in order to change the behavior. ABA specialists work with special needs students, such as children with autism, to help modify behaviors that affect their success in the classroom. Chances are that you will work with specialists and behavior modification programs in your classroom.

Behavior Logs

Ongoing communication with students and parents is essential to effective classroom management. Recurring reports keep parents informed about their child's academic performance and classroom behavior during that long stretch between report cards. Bimonthly or weekly progress reports prevent surprises at report card time for parents and students.

Day-to-day charts

Conduct calendars work well for tracking and communicating the behavior of young students. By stapling a monthly calendar that has large boxes for dates onto a folder, you have an easy tracking system. Assess the student's conduct and record it as a symbol. You can do this immediately after an incident or by the end of the day.

✓ + = Outstanding Behavior   ✓ = Satisfactory Behavior

✓ – = Unsatisfactory Behavior

Weekly behavior charts

I track various behaviors on a small spreadsheet. This behavior chart streamlines my grading system for work habits and behavior. Each child starts the week with 100 points. For each minor infraction or missing homework, I subtract five points. At the end of the week, each student earns a separate grade for work habits and behavior, and the behavior chart is then sent home along with weekly notes and graded papers. Parents sign it, write notes on it to me, and return it with their child.

—Sarah Wolfe Hartman, 3rd-Grade Teacher, Buckland Mills
Elementary School, Gainesville, Virginia

Behavior Log

Behavior Log

Student _____

Date/Time	Behavior Observed	Action Taken

Behavior Management

Classroom and behavior management go hand in hand for a well-run classroom. Procedures and expectations set the stage for managing the classroom and student behaviors. Once the stage is set, teachers must develop rapport with students to affect student behavior and nurture learning. By acting on the five essential behaviors for teachers—acceptance, attention, appreciation, affirmation, and affection (Albert, 1996)—you can establish positive relationships with students. Teachers must go beyond simply accepting students. They must provide them with attention; show appreciation for them; affirm their desirable traits; and show them unconditional affection, kindness, and caring. As part of their behavior management program, some teachers reward positive student behaviors. For additional information about rewards, see **Rewarding Positive Behavior**.

Best Practices

Based on his long-term work with children, educator and child psychologist Ginott (1972) identified various best practices for teachers that significantly impact the learning and behavior of students. His principles, according to Roebuck (2002), "are as pertinent today as they were when his book was first published" (p. 40). Here are Ginott's best practices, along with examples on how to follow them.

- Teacher encourages student cooperation.

   The teacher creates experiences where students work cooperatively on a project.
- Teacher treats students in a dignified manner.

   The teacher never uses sarcasm, yelling, or disrespectful language with students.
- Teacher addresses the situation rather than the student's character.

   In addressing behavioral issues, the teacher makes it clear that he or she is upset with the student's behavior (action or reaction), not the student.
- Teacher never engages in name-calling or negative labeling of students.

   The teacher always addresses the student in a respectful way, such as using the student's first name, and does not refer to students by their academic or social status.
- Teacher never uses sarcasm.

   The teacher does not ask sarcastic questions: "You do know how to read, don't you?"

- Teacher models humane behavior.

  The teacher treats everyone respectfully—even when that level of treatment is not reciprocated.

- Teacher maintains self-control.

  The teacher doesn't scream and yell when angry; the teacher never hits a student.

- Teacher expresses anger appropriately.

  The teacher takes time to calm down and avoids reacting rashly to situations.

- Teacher does not engage in power struggles with students.

  The teacher calmly states facts to avoid a back and forth argument about a situation.

- Teacher allows face-saving exits to help students maintain their dignity.

  The teacher privately addresses problems so that no one else is aware of the situation.

> **❝** *I've come to the frightening conclusion that I am the decisive element in the classroom. It's my daily mood that makes the weather. As a teacher, I possess a tremendous power to make a child's life miserable or joyous. I can be a tool of torture or an instrument of inspiration. I can humiliate or humor, hurt or heal. In all situations, it is my response that decides whether a crisis will be escalated or de-escalated and a child humanized or de-humanized.*
>
> —Haim Ginott, Teacher, Psychologist, and Child Therapist (1922–1973) **❞**

Body Language

Your body language speaks volumes and can convey a message without a word from you. Two effective uses of body language are the "silent treatment" and the "teacher look." To get a student's attention, stop speaking and whatever you are doing in that moment to look straight at the student who is being disruptive. Do not waiver, even if it takes a few moments for the student to realize that all attention is focused his or her way. Once the student glances your way, simply shake your head a bit to communicate that his or her actions are inappropriate. Then, without words spoken, you and the class can calmly return to the task at hand.

How near you are to a student, or a student to you, strongly conveys a message as well. See **Propinquity** and **Proximity** for details.

Boundaries

It is easy to take for granted that students are well aware of boundaries but, once again, assume nothing! Clarifying boundaries in your classroom ensures that you and the students are on the same page. Start with basic concepts, as with these recommended boundaries:

- Have students call you by a formal name, not your first name, to maintain a distinct line of professionalism.
- Do not allow students to put one another down.
- Let each student have individual space in the classroom.
- Determine from the beginning how much students will know about your personal life.

It is wise to set boundaries for parent–teacher interactions as well. Setting boundaries for situations involving parents shows professionalism and will increase your confidence for conferences, volunteers in the classroom, and calls home. To help you set these boundaries, consider the following questions.

- Do you want parents to call you by a formal name or your first name?
- Do you want parents to call you at home?
- Do you want parents to make an appointment to speak with you?
- How much personal information do you want parents to know?

For more information on relationships with students and parents, see specific alpha entries, such as **Parents, Parent–Teacher Conferences, Friending Students,** and **Open House.**

Broken Record Technique

This technique is very effective, particularly with older students. It is not unusual for a student to argue with the teacher when his or her behavior is being corrected. Many teachers make the mistake of entering into the argument, creating a tug-of-war between teacher and student. Rather than enter this no-win battle, use the broken record technique. This technique entails continually stating the facts and the rules being broken without responding to the student's argumentative phrases. The broken record technique keeps the focus on rules and the power with the teacher.

You sound like a broken record

Teacher: "Stop passing notes, Sue."

Sue: "I didn't pass a note."

Teacher: "In this class, notes are not passed. Conversation waits until an appropriate time."

Sue: "I didn't pass a note."

Teacher: "In this class, notes are not passed."

Sue: "Do you see a note? Who did I pass it to?"

Teacher: "In this class, notes are not passed."

Sue: "You are seeing things."

Teacher: "In this class, notes are not passed."

Sue: "You always pick on me."

Teacher: "In this class, notes are not passed."

Sue: "Whatever."

Bulletin Boards

Some teachers love to do bulletin boards; others do not. Whether or not you enjoy designing bulletin boards, they can be time-consuming. Student-generated boards, however, make great projects and learning experiences while saving you time. Try one or more of these board ideas listed here.

Student of the Week. Set up one bulletin board for "Student of the Week." Weekly choose a student's name at random for that week's board. By the way, students usually enjoy making a big deal out of this random drawing. One educator plays a recorded drumroll before announcing the name every Friday afternoon. You can take a digital picture of that student for the bulletin board or have the student bring in a current picture, along with other items. The chosen student then takes home four 8 × 10" sheets of construction paper and a letter for the family. All you have to do is pull the letter from a packet you already have prepared. Your letter might look something like this one.

Student of the Week Letter

Dear Parent,

We have great news! Your child is next week's Student of the Week!
This is a great reward and source of pride for most students, as all
week long a bulletin board will display their interests, hobbies, and
favorite things.

This designation means _____ is the star of the class all
week. Because you know your child best, please help your child to
create four posters to place on the Student of the Week bulletin board.
Use the paper provided as follows:

- Yellow sheet—favorite foods (*may list them or
  attach pictures*)

- White sheet—a drawing (*by the student*) of your family,
  including pets

- Blue sheet—sports and hobbies (*draw or paste pictures*)

- Green sheet—"free-to-choose" poster for anything your child
  would like to share

Remember, I will post these sheets on the bulletin board on Monday
and return the sheets to you on Friday.

Thank you for your help in creating a special week for your child.

Sincerely,
(*Sign each one individually.*)

On Monday morning, allow the student to share these sheets as they are posted on the bulletin board. You too should have a bulletin board. To help students know you, make yourself "Star of the Week" for the first week of school.

Interesting news. Display an "In the News" bulletin board for weekly news coverage in your classroom. After lining a bulletin board with newspaper, have assigned students find an interesting news story to share briefly with the class. The stories, from the newspaper, online articles, classroom news, or school newsletters, are then tacked on the "In the News" board and cleared at the end of the week for the next week's stories.

Quick-change board. Mount clear plastic sleeves on the wall outside your classroom to display student work. Two clear sheet protectors, a clear bag, or a pocket folder work well for displaying work, and no staples or staple pullers are needed. Artwork and star–worthy papers simply slide in and out of these display cases.

Interactive boards. Interactive bulletin boards display participatory activities for students, from creating an item for the board or solving math problems to reading a QR code to learn more about the subject presented.

Don't forget the walls just outside your classroom! Attractive hallway displays energize your students and show parents and your school community that your classroom is a productive environment.

Bullying

Did you know that 1 in 4 students in grades K–12 is bullied, 1 in 5 students admits to some form of bullying, and every 7 minutes a child is bullied on the playground? These survey statistics, from the Stomp Out Bullying site (http://stompoutbullying. com/aboutbullying_theissue.php) are compelling evidence for schools and teachers to provide bullying prevention strategies and combat various types of bullying.

What is bullying? Batsche and Knoff (1994) described bullying as "a form of aggression in which one or more students physically and/or psychologically (and more recently, sexually) harass another student repeatedly over a period of time" (p. 166). Bullies desire power, are typically antisocial, and appear to gain satisfaction from the harassment of others.

Described further, bullying involves a real or perceived power imbalance with actions that include threats, spreading rumors, attacking someone physically or verbally, and intentionally excluding someone from a group (U.S. Department of Health and Human Services, 2012).

Addressing bullying. The ideal way to address bullying is to take preventative measures. Begin the year with a No Tolerance Policy on bullying, clearly identifying to students what constitutes bullying. Learn your school's policies and procedures regarding harassment and follow those regulations implicitly. If your school doesn't have a policy, set specific classroom rules about and consequences for bullying, and carry them out immediately. Too often, teachers look the other way or view bullying as a rite of passage; but school violence is an issue too serious to ignore.

Giving students opportunities to learn empathy and effective communication techniques can help prevent bullying. Simulation exercises, such as "Playing the Bully," promote empathy. Also helpful is to encourage parents and students to limit exposure to violence and to structure time away from school so that it is spent under appropriate supervision.

Playing the bully

In this role-play, students act out a situation in which one student is singled out and harassed by a few bullies. When creating the simulation, be sure the chosen victim's ridiculed characteristic cannot be associated specifically with anyone in your class. Students are quick to make inferences. Following the simulation, encourage students to discuss how the victim feels and what motives might have been behind the bullies' actions.

Victims of bullies also need help with their behaviors. Teach them strategies for dealing with bullies and have them practice assertiveness through role-playing. Use special programs on character building, peer mediation, and bully prevention accessible through your school, stores, or on the Internet. For additional reading and program sources, see **Resources** in the **Extras** section of this book.

Another way to address this difficult topic is with stories that promote empathy or build confidence. You can read children's books about bullying to the class and make them available in your classroom library.

Burnout

Hooks (in Preskill & Jacobvitz, 2001) referred to burnout as a "concomitant risk for those who aspire to create excitement in their classrooms" (p. 174). Burnout can happen subtly and too easily to caring teachers. Don't wait until you need a remedy to seek solutions. Establish a healthy balance of work and play to stay vital. Have a life outside the classroom, and don't become all-consumed with your job. Share your challenges and concerns with colleagues when needed and tend to your well-being. See **Take Time to . . .** for tips on keeping healthy in body, mind, and soul.

NO SHE'S NOT BURNING OUT — SHE'S JUST ON FIRE FOR TEACHING!

Call-Outs

Call-outs are disruptive to a lesson. To prevent them, first examine why they are happening. Are you inadvertently promoting them? If you accept a call-out, then you have reinforced them and they will continue to occur. Many teachers don't realize they are accepting call-outs because once in the flow of the lesson, they do not notice. During a lesson, stop and ask yourself, "Was that a call-out"? If it was, then ignore the student, model the raised hand sign, and call on a student whose hand is raised.

Capable, Connected, and Contributing

When students feel capable and connected, and contribute in the classroom, they acquire a sense of belonging, with feeling capable coming first (Albert, 1989; 1996). A classroom atmosphere where mistakes are viewed as learning opportunities encourages a sense of capability and boosts confidence. Connection is second; students must feel connected to their classmates and their teachers. Last, students must believe they are contributing to their worlds—the classroom and beyond. Community service and peer assistance present various opportunities through which students can contribute.

Cartoon Drawing

An instructional strategy that helps some students work through their behavior is cartoon drawing. Having students draw a cartoon depicting events leading to the poor behavior gives them an opportunity to show the choice made and then rewrite it (or in this case, draw it) so that a better choice is shown as well.

Cell Phones

Though lower elementary students may not have cell phones, the age at which children get mobile phones is getting increasingly younger. Be prepared before any cell phone incidents by establishing rules for them at the beginning of the year, especially if you plan to use them as learning tools. Follow and base your classroom rules on the school policy. School policies generally fall in these two categories:

- Cell phones are banned on school property. If a student is caught with a cell phone, it becomes confiscated and the parent must come to pick it up.
- Cell phones may be on school property, but may not be used or visible to other students.

What about your cell phone policy? Teachers should not use their cell phones in their classroom when students are present. Teaching is hard work and requires your focus at all times.

Chairs

Are "wiggle warts" simply tired of the lesson? Students squirming in their seats may indicate something besides boredom with a lesson. It may be their chairs. Think about it. Have you ever been in a sitting position where your feet didn't touch the floor? If so you probably swung your legs or scooted forward to touch your toes to the floor. Students come in all sizes, but do their chairs? When chairs are not the right size, students wrap their feet around the legs of the chair for stability, sit forward without back support (which is tiring and causes wiggles), or sit back and swing their feet. When they do, unnecessary classroom movement distracts instructional time. By individualizing chair and desk size, you can minimize at least some unnecessary classroom movement. Students also get restless when their posture is poor. Encourage correct posture, not only for keeping them alert but also to promote their overall health. To help them remember good posture, you may want to put up a poster similar to one found at Living Posture (www.livingposture.com/article/13/posters).

Cheating

The best way to deal with cheating is to take strategic actions to prevent it. During testing, seating should be arranged so that seeing another student's responses is difficult. Help students do their own work by increasing space between desks or using "personal privacy walls." Prior to testing, be sure to communicate clearly your policy about cheating, as in the following example.

Teacher: "Today I want to find out how well YOU can spell this week's vocabulary words. You have worked hard all week to learn these words and now you have a chance to show me how much you learned. I need you to stay focused on your own work. Try not to let your eyes wander to anyone else's paper. If you copy something from someone else, that doesn't help any of us. It doesn't tell me what you learned, and it is a wrong thing to do because you would be stealing someone else's work. I trust you to be honest and show me what you have learned."

Choices and Consequences

Choice in behavior management is less about offering multiple options and more about informing students of the expectation or rule and the consequence for not following it. By presenting your expectations for a change in student behavior and the result of not changing, you place the responsibility for a decision to change (or not) with the student. Options in a disciplining situation empower students; and, remember, the desire for power is often behind many misbehaviors (Dreikurs, Cassel, & Ferguson, 2004). Also see **Attention**.

Most people like to feel they are in control, and students are no different. Therefore, when possible, give the student two choices—both of which work for you as well. This choice gives the student the locus of control.

> *Teacher*: "You have two choices. You may finish your work quietly at your desk, or you may move to the "Quiet Desk" (a spot away from others but within view of the teacher) to complete your work."
>
> *Student*: "I'll stay here."
>
> *Teacher*: "Okay. You have chosen to stay here. Now if you do not complete your work quietly, the consequence is ..."

Successful classroom management requires consequences to follow broken rules and poor behavior choices. Consequences, according to Albert's *Cooperative Discipline* (1989; 1996), must be respectful, reasonable, related to the offense, and reliably enforced in order to be valuable. First, the consequence must be *related* to the offense; there must be a logical connection between the two. Second, the consequence must be *reasonable;* its main purpose should be to teach value rather than punish students. Third, the consequence should be *respectful*, allowing the student to maintain dignity. Last, the consequence must be *reliably enforced* so students know that you stand by your word. Doing what you say you'll do is essential to successful management using choice and consequences. Students will test you, so be prepared to carry out a consequence. They test teachers because their past experiences have shown them that fighting a consequence leads to giving in by the person awarding the consequence. Do not be that person. When they learn you do not cave, they stop trying.

Valuable consequence

Justin is rocking back his chair, again. Whether or not you find this habit annoying, it is potentially hazardous, and so you state the problem to him and ask him to stop leaning his chair back. You explain that you don't want him to fall backward and get hurt. If the behavior continues, tell Justin the consequences of not stopping: "Justin, if you continue to rock backward, you will lose the privilege of sitting in that chair."

You have just given a consequence *related to the offense* that is also a *reasonable request* from which Justin can learn to change while maintaining dignity (*respectful*). If Justin continues to rock his chair, you must deliver the consequences given to him for the rule to become *reliably enforced*. Delivering consequences stated shows Justin—and his classmates—that you mean what you say. Before you give a consequence, be sure you can carry it out. In Justin's case, losing his chair means moving to a chair he cannot rock, standing for five minutes or, perhaps, sitting on the floor.

—Pam Kramer Ertel, Co-author, *The ABC's of Classroom Management*

Choices for Learning

Choices stimulate creativity and generate opportunities. At any grade level, allowing student choice acknowledges various learning styles and intelligences within the classroom and demonstrates respect for the individual. Giving assignment choices or options in how a project is completed is motivating for students, because they can follow their natural abilities or desires to accomplish an assignment. Offering several choices for an assignment may take a little creative planning and assessment, but the time and effort result in motivated students excited about the task. And, remember, motivated students yield a well-managed classroom.

When presenting choices, you will need a structural foundation supporting the choices. That's where rubrics come in. At the beginning of a project, present your expectations, evaluation criteria, and rubrics that define the levels of student achievement. Choice does not mean "anything goes." Successful choices start with clear expectations and support.

Class Meetings

Regularly scheduled class meetings build community and offer a great setting to address problems affecting the majority of students in your classroom. Class meetings are also a great time to engage students in meaningful problem solving. To ensure effective meetings, establish clear rules at the first session. Incorporate activities during the meetings and within your classroom to build trust, respect, and community. You can use the following guidelines for your class meetings.

In class meetings, *do* ...
- teach students to use I-statements and to speak in general terms. Avoid using specific names. For example, "I noticed someone cutting in line today," or "I had trouble working because of loud talking."

- set aside a specific block of time for discussions. The amount of time will vary according to the age of the students.
- allow anyone to speak who has a concern.
- facilitate meetings and model procedures during the first few sessions.
- establish a time limit for the session.
- take time to review behavioral expectations, especially in preparation for special events such as field trips, guest speakers, assemblies, and activity-based learning experiences.

But during meetings, *do not* ...

- allow students to identify students by name when discussing a problem (keep it general.)
- permit put-downs.
- ignore or change the meeting time unless absolutely necessary.
- let anyone dominate the discussion.
- permit foul or disrespectful language or behavior.
- allow students to get off track.

Classroom Climate

What do you want the atmosphere of your student community to be like? How can it be enjoyable and learning focused? You are the "weather" director; you have tremendous power to influence classroom climate. As you think about your room's climate and how it can be achieved, consider the following questions.

How will you instill a love for learning in students?

- What will you communicate to students about the value of learning?
- How can you encourage engagement in the learning process?

How will you create a culture of respect?

- What behaviors will you model for students?
- What rules will you establish to foster respect for everyone in your class?
- What consequences will you give when students don't act respectfully?

How will you make students feel welcome, especially at the start of the year?

- How will you greet students?
- How can you quickly learn the names of your students?
- What can you do to show students you care about them?

Classroom Management Plan

Developing your plan. When developing your classroom management plan, focus first on strategies that encourage and affirm positive behavior. Establish brief, simple rules that help create an environment conducive to learning. Accompany them with constructive consequences. Your plan should reflect your beliefs about learning and, most importantly, help children learn to manage their own behaviors. The most effective plans usually include student input. Students are more likely to buy into a plan that makes sense to them and to which they've contributed. Besides, students have great ideas for creating an outstanding learning environment. You'll be amazed! How you introduce your management plan is important, so plan carefully. Students accept governing better when they understand the rationale behind the rules and their consequences. Your management plan also should identify basic classroom procedures (see **Procedures Pave the Way**).

Sharing your plan. Parents need a copy of your classroom rules. Building a partnership with parents begins with knowledge and clear expectations. When they know your rules and the rationale behind them, they are empowered with knowledge about your expectations for their children. You have also helped build trust.

A good time to discuss your management plan is during the first Open House or back-to-school night. Your principal also needs a copy of your management plan. Having your plan on file benefits you and the administrators, especially if you should have to call on the principal to back you up on a management issue. Sharing your plan with your students' instructors for art, music, and physical education informs them about what you already have established and gives you "extra eyes and ears." Surprisingly, students rarely consider that teachers communicate and share concerns about their students.

> *Don't take behavior management issues person-*
> *ally. It is easy to feel as though behaviors in your*
> *classroom are a direct reflection of you as a teach-*
> *er; that you are somehow deficient in management*
> *techniques or strategies. Understand, rather, that*
> *human behavior is difficult to manage and that*
> *collaboration is often the best strategy.*
>   —Maegan McCord, Learning Support
>   K–2, Gilbertsville Elementary,
>   Boyertown, PA

Closet Catastrophes—Prevented

The classroom closet is as prone to the same clutter catastrophes as home closets—probably more so. Just multiply one coat, book bag, lunchbox, hat, and a pair of mittens by the number of students in your classroom to calculate the potential catastrophe! With a good system, however, you and your students can keep the closet organized and trips to it orderly.

Closet catastrophe prevention

1. Assign each student a hook, hanger, or specific area to hang a coat, labeling it with a name or number to designate to whom it belongs.
2. Use the same system to identify where lunchboxes are stored. If additional storage areas are needed, continue the system there as well.

3. Add labeled bins in the closet area where students can store hats, lunchboxes, extra shoes, and sweaters. Contained items keep the closet neat and clean.

4. Request that parents put their student's name on all possessions and personal items. Name labels prevent mix-ups among possessions, which helps prevent arguments and a big concern among teachers—lice! Of course, there are safety concerns, especially for young students, so be sure to encourage parents to put the child's name inside the clothing, bags, hats, and books to eliminate strangers calling the students by name.

Communication

You teach; you are a communicator. You communicate information, ideas, plans, expectations, news, and requests. You communicate to people and with people—in individual meetings with students, conferences with parents, conversations with colleagues, and in newsletters, notes, emails, and phone calls with the constituents of your school community. As a multitasking, multi-level, minute-to-minute communicator, you need to communicate efficiently and effectively. Managing communications goes hand in hand with managing your classroom, student behavior, and paperwork.

Strive for clarity and conciseness in your messages, conveying a professional, yet agreeable manner. Use proper styles, grammar, and spelling in your written communiqués. Speak clearly when leaving voice mails and include a contact number and the best time to reach you. Let your written and spoken words set the stage for a positive rapport between you and the receiver. For information, suggestions, and details on different forms of communication, see related categories such as **Newsletters**, **Notes Home**, and **Parents**.

Contracts

Older students respond well to behavior contracts. A behavior contract states the desired action, the consequence for not performing the desired action, the amount of time the contract is to be used (reasonable and developmentally appropriate to students' age), any rewards, and the signatures of all parties. A sample contract is shown here.

Behavior Contract

Behavior Contract

I _____ will do the following:

_____

_____

_____

_____

If I do these things, I will earn

_____

_____

_____

_____

If I choose not to do these things, this will happen:

_____

_____

_____

_____

I will review this contract again on _____

Student signature _____

Teacher signature _____

Cooperation vs. Competition

Should classrooms encourage cooperation or competition? What does your classroom look like? The difference is quite important. Imagine a boat sinking and only one lifejacket is available to the two passengers. In competition the boaters fight over who wears the life jacket; in cooperation they both hold onto a side of the jacket and float together. That is not to say that competition is bad. There is a place for it, and having both competition and cooperation in the classroom establishes balance.

Competition. How competitive is your classroom? Do your students often participate in spelling bees, "mad-minute" math races, and other similarly styled learning games? Though these activities sharpen skills and encourage quick thinking, they also tend to promote perceptions of who is "smart" and who is "dumb." Students who do not excel academically or who have a learning disability typically find these games to be torturous. In fact, to avoid these activities, these students often act out, creating behavior problems. Even students who do well in competitive games may be adverse to them. They may be sensitive to those less inclined to do well or are shy enough to dislike the public attention.

Choose, instead, activities through which students compete against themselves or work with others toward a common goal. When students compete against themselves, they are more likely to build personal confidence. The goal of a mad-minute math drill, for example, is for a student to best the time of the previous drill.

Cooperation. For cooperative endeavors, students can work on projects or assignments in groups or participate in team learning. Teams-Games-Tournament, or TGT, is the prototype for cooperative learning developed by Slavin (DeVries & Slavin, 1978) in which students work together to improve members of the teams. Competition occurs between team members of equal abilities. That is, academically high-achieving students compete against one another and students who struggle in the area of "competition" work with one another to bring equal amounts of points back to the team.

Cultural Differences

Students whose cultures differ from your own or the area in which you teach may exhibit conduct that comes across as misbehavior, but may be the norm in their culture of origin. For example, sharing answers in Russia and Eastern Europe is acceptable because "the good of the many is more important than the individual." Being aware of cultural differences can help you form culturally respectful responses to questionable student behavior in the classroom. According to Bartzis and Hayner (2009), the following cultural norms may underlie some students' behaviors.

Cultures around the world

Russia and Eastern Europe
- Sharing notes and talking in class are okay and not hidden.
- Classroom goals are to bring the whole class level up.

Germany
- Sharing answers is common.
- Not sharing is considered a social taboo.

Mexico
- Sharing is common, but students deny it.
- Professors do not expect citations in paper.

Costa Rica
- Teamwork is the rule in personal and academic life, including supporting those who do not contribute to the group.

China
- Intellectual property is a foreign concept.
- Saving face and maintaining group harmony are society values.

Burma
- Student learning is seen as a task shared by the group.
- Selfishness and pursuing personal goals at the expense of others is unacceptable.

India and Bangladesh
- Students have rioted when cheating on tests is prevented.
- Exams should not be memory tests.

Greece
- Focus is on learning concepts rather than words.
- Connecting quotes demonstrates understanding.

Cursing

What if a student uses inappropriate language in the classroom? You can punish the offender and render a consequence, but it may be more productive to give the student the opportunity to "expand" his or her vocabulary bank and use alternative words. When a student curses or uses a phrase inappropriate to the classroom, simply ask the student to rephrase the statement into more acceptable language. This exercise teaches students how to adapt their speech and actions to various environments.

Student: "This sucks."

Teacher: "That type of language is not acceptable at school. Give me three ways in acceptable language to say the same thing."

Student: "This is terrible"

Teacher: "Great. That's one way."

Student: "I don't like this."

Teacher: "You are now thinking of acceptable language. You have one left."

Student: "This isn't fun."

Teacher: "Good work. Now you have more acceptable ways of expressing yourself."

Custody and Divorce

For children's safety and your liability, you need to know about custody concerns surrounding your students, whether stemming from a divorce or another situation. Be aware of the people who can legally have access to your students. Your school probably requires parents to file a copy in the school office of any custody agreements concerning their child. A custody agreement gives the legal arrangements for the child, saying who has custody and when. It also tells who can access school information. It is important for you to be aware of this information and any rulings about sharing academic information with noncustodial parents. For an interesting article on custody paperwork, see http://ncinfo.iog.unc.edu/pubs/electronicversions/slb/slbwin04/article2.pdf. Though this article applies to North Carolina, its content is beneficial for all to consider.

Cyberbullying

The extensive use of social media and cell phones means that the reach of bullying is far more pervasive than in the school hallways or on playgrounds. It's a serious problem and, as a role model to students, you can impact prevention and intervention. First know your school district's policy regarding cyberbullying; there can be legal ramifications. Also become familiar with your school's prevention program—prevention is the best remedy. Model respectful behaviors and apply the following community building and prevention strategies (Strom & Strom, 2005).

Develop community, prevent bullying

1. Establish a no-teasing policy. Help students understand the negative impact of teasing.
2. Work continually to create a welcoming classroom climate where students feel like they belong.
3. Remind students that name-calling, eye-rolling, or laughing at peers will not be tolerated in your classroom.
4. Develop a glossary of words students are not to use when they talk about one another.
5. Teach and model conflict resolution strategies and have students practice them in specific activities. Skills needed include: (a) ability to develop alternative solutions to a problem; (b) understanding of the connection between means and ends; (c) capacity to assess consequences of an action or decision; and (d) capability of selecting the best solution to a problem (Broadbear & Broadbear, 2000).

Daily Agenda

Begin each day with a very effective instructional strategy by posting the day's tasks in a prominent place. Whether you use a whiteboard near the classroom entrance, the main board, or another visible space, the daily agenda should be part of students' routine. This agenda includes a daily independent task, or morning work, that students begin when they arrive to class (see **Daily Task**).

The reason a posted agenda is an effective teaching tool is that it gives students ownership in the daily process. They can take responsibility for accomplishing the day's work rather than relying on teacher direction. You may want to give an incentive for completing tasks and reaching the agenda's goals. Many students enjoy in-class "free time" as a reward.

Daily agenda

8:30–8:45 Morning Work, Pledge, Announcement

8:45–10:00 Reading Groups

    Group A = *The Hungry Hippo*, pp. 46–53; workbook, pp. 33–35

    Group B = *Into the Darkness*, pp. 36–40; workbook, pp. 28–29

    Group C = *High above the Clouds*, pp. 45–49; pp. 19 and 22

10:00–10:40 Activity (PE)

10:40–11:30 Social Studies, pp. 57–60

11:30–12:00 Lunch

Daily Task

Get students engaged and set the tone of the classroom for the day with a morning activity written on an overhead, blackboard, or easel near the door. Seeing a set task as they enter the classroom helps students quickly transition to the day's agenda. Daily tasks work best when students can easily jump in and do the work in 5–10 minutes, without asking questions of you or their classmates. Vary lesson review worksheets, word problems, brief writing exercises, and daily language activities throughout the week. You also can warm up students' brains with a puzzle or brainteaser.

Defiant Students

Defiant students may challenge you in ways that trigger a rise in your blood pressure. You want to maintain your composure, yet there's nothing more annoying than a student who not only defies your authority, but also does it with attitude! Nevertheless, it is important (and healthier) that you do not lose your cool; act rather than react.

When a student refuses to follow your directive, pause to think about your next step. Your response may determine whether or not the situation escalates or turns into something more serious, perhaps even dangerous. Make every effort to keep your emotions in check and avoid engaging in a power struggle with the student. This situation demands your calmness, maturity, and creative problem-solving skills. Stay focused on the goal you want to achieve, and then work toward meeting that goal. Don't let your ego get in the way of your clear thinking.

Actions to take. Set a time to discuss privately with the student his or her defiant behavior, preferably after sufficient cool-down time. Let the student know that though you are not addressing the behavior at that time, it will be discussed later. Deliver a firm closing statement that summarizes what happened and identifies when the two of you will meet to discuss the incident: "I understand that you are refusing to sit down at your desk. Is this correct? We will discuss this problem during your recess time."

Be sure to follow through and conduct the meeting with the student. When you discuss the problem, analyze the events leading up to the situation and explore ways to prevent recurrences of the problem. Deliver consequences when necessary. If at any time you do not feel safe meeting alone with the student, you must call in the parents, a colleague, or an administrator. To prevent getting caught in a verbal power struggle, see **Broken Record Technique**.

Keeping it calm

Maintain a calm demeanor to moderate the situation and prevent triggering further bad behavior. Because certain behaviors can escalate defiant behavior, be sure not to:

- raise your voice
- use sarcasm
- touch the student
- debate the situation
- stand too close to the student (don't get in his or her face)
- humiliate or mock the student

Democratic Classroom

Though democracy in classrooms is advocated, it is not always practiced. Giving choice to students, however, brings democracy to life (also see **Choices and Consequences**). When students take part in planning lessons, decorating the room, and solving problems that arise, they participate in the democratic process.

If, for example, two students deface school property, they can work together to decide the best way to right the wrong. Problems affecting the entire class, though, should be solved by the whole class (see **Class Meetings**).

Realize that consensus is not the goal. All students may not agree on the same thing at the same time; but through this process, they experience how working and deciding together can result in a safer, more interesting school life. Let your classroom be the place where students learn they have an important voice. Give them choice opportunities so they can learn in the classroom how to contribute to society as a whole.

Desks

Play area. Sometimes students pay more attention to items in their desk than they do listening to the lesson. When this happens in your classroom, either move the student to a table, placing his or her desk items in a laundry basket to the side, or reverse the desk so that the opening is away from the student.

Clean and tidy desks. Students' desks can get very messy—inside and out—but cleaning them does not have to be a chore. A fun way to clean desks (and learn) is to turn the desktops into a shaving cream writing board for lesson-related activities. Simply place a small mound of shaving cream on each student's desk that is spread into a thin layer. Ask questions related to your lesson or give math problems or spelling words and have students write their answers on their "shaving cream tablets." Do check for student allergies first. Also, for students who have tactile issues, as children with autism often do, supply latex-free disposable rubber gloves. When done, students wipe off the desks with paper towels and dispose of them in the trash can.

Now for the scariest part of students' desks—the inside! Ensure the possibility of clean desk awards with weekly cleanouts that begin with specific directions rather than the announcement "It's time to clean out your desks." Try prompts such as "Take out your reading book and place it on your desk. Now take out your math book and folder, and put them on your desk. What is left in your desk? Are there papers? They need to go home today. If you have loose items such as pencils and markers, please organize them." Expect full trash cans!

If you wonder how your students can find anything in their desks, even with regular cleaning, it may be time for alternate storage. To help students retrieve items quickly and easily, store infrequently used textbooks and distribute only when needed. Students also can use "chair pockets" to hold homework folders and lessons as another way to prevent crowded desks.

Digital Citizenship

Managing a classroom, as this book shows you, encompasses many aspects of classroom life, including handling student behaviors, developing and reinforcing routines and rules, planning lessons, organizing materials, and building relationships. Guiding students in learning various technology tools and how to use them safely, effectively, and responsibly is part of managing a classroom. Digital literacy in its many forms is absolutely necessary for 21st-century students, which means this knowledge and its delivery is essential for you, a 21st-century teacher.

In its 2010 report, *Youth Safety on a Living Internet*, The Online Safety and Technology Working Group (OSTWG) advocated that educators "in the process of teaching regular subjects, teach the constructive, mindful use of social media enabled by digital citizenship and new-media literacy training" (p. 20). Learn about your school's digital citizenship program and integrate it into your lessons and daily discussions. If your school does not follow a specific program, begin with a few of the nine elements suggested in "Digital Citizenship for Educational Change" (Ribble, 2012). You can learn more about digital citizenship and your role through resource sites such as International Society for Technology in Education (www.iste.org/standards/nets-for-teachers).

Digital basics

Digital communication: electronic exchange of information

Digital literacy: process of teaching and learning about technology and its use

Digital etiquette: electronic standards of conduct or procedure

Digital law: electronic responsibility for actions and deeds

Digital security (self-protection): electronic precautions to guarantee safety

Direct—Don't Ask

Be careful not to ask rhetorical questions. So often teachers prompt students to take an action with questions such as "Would everyone please take out a pencil?" when the intention is "Take out a pencil." The semantics may be minor, but the difference in results is major. Requests give students the option of responding "yes" or "no." Give choices when available, but direct or command when no options are involved. Watch for this pattern in your requests and remind yourself to direct rather than ask.

Directory Information

Remember that the only information teachers can share with other students and parents is called *directory information.* This data includes student's name, address, telephone number, date and place of birth, honors and awards, and dates of attendance. Under the Family Educational Rights and Privacy Act (FERPA), parents or guardians have the option of blocking the release of this information. Schools are annually required to notify parents and eligible students of their rights under FERPA, but the method of notification is at the school's discretion. To protect confidentiality and honor students' rights, it is important for you to know who has blocked directory information.

Discipline

> *Good discipline is a series of little victories in which a teacher, through small decencies, reaches a child's heart.*
>
> —Haim Ginott, Teacher, Psychologist, and Child Therapist (1922–1973)

Discipline often carries a negative connotation, but it really shouldn't. Charles (2005) defined *discipline* as "what teachers do to help students behave acceptably in school" (p. 2). Discipline includes both rewards and penalties or consequences. Wong and Wong (2005) identified three key components of a discipline plan: rules, consequences, and rewards. Teaching students how to behave appropriately is an essential part of your job. Accept this role and do not expect your students to enter your classroom with all behavior skills and courtesies mastered. Check **Resources** in the **Extras** section for resources on classroom discipline.

Dismissals with Dignity

The end of the school day is important. It is a time to review what was learned during the day and to leave the room in a calm and orderly manner. Dismissal time, however, can be quite chaotic as students busily gather homework, books, coats, and last-minute notes for home to make their bus on time. While directing students, teachers also may be listening to office announcements regarding students, buses, and reminders. Organized dismissals are essential!

Plan for dismissal as you would a lesson. Allow ample time to review the day, clean up, gather items to go home, and leave in an orderly fashion. Engage students in a calm activity, such as a story or whole-class review of the day's learning, before they need to pack up. A settling task sets the tone for a composed dismissal.

Remember, when teachers provide a well-organized dismissal, students leave with dignity rather than in a chaotic rush amid yelled departure instructions. These strategies lead to dignified dismissals:

- End instruction early enough to allow sufficient preparation time for dismissal. Elementary students need about 15 minutes to get ready.
- Create a methodical system for coat and book bag retrieval, wherever they are housed. Calling students by their bus number in the order buses leave works well.
- Post homework assignments on the board to help students easily gather any and all materials needed to complete the assignments (also see **Homework**).
- Distribute take-home items in student mailboxes well before dismissal, with mailbox checks part of the dismissal routine.

A final and vital word about dismissal. awareness. Be aware of your school's policy regarding dismissal changes for individual students. For example, if a parent leaves a message that "Johnny is to ride with Sue's mom today instead of taking the bus," it should be verified. Schools and teachers must be aware of these situations so they do not release a child to a noncustodial parent or stranger.

Displays

Always exhibit student work in your classroom. Each student should have representative work on display when at all possible. Presenting the work about which they are most proud acknowledges students and gives them visibility to others. Recognition through displayed work is especially important to those students who are quiet. When students help determine items to be displayed, you create another opportunity for choice in the classroom.

Embarrassing Moments

How you handle embarrassing moments can build rapport with students as well as your own confidence. For example, what would you do if, in the middle of a lesson, you accidently let out a big belch—or worse—and the students go crazy? Some teachers might yell at the students to quiet down, glare at them, or pretend nothing happened. One teacher who had this happen to her decided that acknowledging the incident with humor was the best way to move forward. So she just laughed and said in her best exaggerated voice, "Did I do that? Excuse me!" The students laughed with her and they returned to the lesson. Addressing the embarrassment shows your humanity and allows you to model appropriate responses for students. Simply stating facts or using humor manages the situation in a professional manner and helps everyone return to the task at hand.

Emergency Procedures

A situation during my early teaching years made me realize how vital it is to be prepared for emergencies. While walking behind a line of students, one student suddenly dropped out of line, fell to the floor, and began to shake violently. Fortunately, I had some training in medical procedures and knew what to do. Would you? First, consider taking or organizing at your school a Red Cross First Aid and CPR course. Second, learn your school's procedures for emergencies. If your school does not have a procedure, help to create one. When developing an emergency procedure plan, consider the following questions:

- How will you call for help? Is there a classroom nearby where someone could hear you? What about on the playground?
- Who determines whether an ambulance should be called?
- How will other students or bystanders (potential gawkers) be removed from the area? Who assumes responsibility for them?
- Who obtains emergency contact information and contacts the parents?
- How will you direct the ambulance to the specific accident site? Precious time is lost when the ambulance driver or the attendants don't know where to go. For accidents on the playground, station one person at the entrance to the school to direct the ambulance.
- Where is the information on student allergies? Who gets those records and takes them to the accident site?
- Who rides in the ambulance with the student? How does this faculty or staff person get home from the hospital?

Energy Issues

We are not talking about heating and cooling or global warming here, but rather the dynamics in your classroom. Former educator and author Jon Gordon identified 10 rules to fuel any group with positive energy in his bestseller *The Energy Bus* (2007). His focus on positive energy has helped leaders from all walks of life (including educators) transform their environments so that those people in them experience more success, happiness, better performance, and more teamwork. Your classroom environment and its energy greatly influence classroom management—and you are its Chief Energy Officer (Gordon, 2007).

As the leader and role model, you impact tremendously the overall energy level (high or low) in the classroom environment. Emotions are contagious, and your positive attitude and energy can have a significant impact on the enthusiasm, energy, motivation, and mood of your students and the flow of your classroom.

You don't have to be a Type A or Energizer Bunny® personality to fill the role of Chief Energy Officer; you simply make use of positive energy to inspire others, accomplish tasks, and handle challenges. You quickly dispel negativity, complaints, and actions that drain you and your students of positive energy. Energy usually generates energy and positive approaches; but if you should ever need your batteries charged, refer to **Wellness** in this book.

SOLAR ENERGY... HAS NOTHING ON KINDERGARTNERS!

Environment

Just as location is crucial in real estate, so is classroom environment in student engagement and learning. From wall décor and colors to desk or table arrangements, various features of your classroom influence students and their learning. As director, designer, and choreographer of your classroom, it's up to you to create a place that is conducive to learning: a safe and secure space where students can grow. How will you create an optimal learning environment?

Appearance. Start with the room's physical appearance. Is your classroom welcoming and comfortable? Think about the ages of your students and imagine their reactions to the room. Sit at several student desks and the various centers you develop to get a "kid perspective." Encourage a calm atmosphere with the use of soft colors, especially blue. Avoid getting too mellow; you still want to stimulate students' desire to learn. Kindle curiosity and promote learning through interesting materials, decorations, and activity centers. For suggestions on staging your classroom, see the **Environment Checklist** in the **Extras** section of this book.

Tone. Next, think about how your personality can shape the classroom environment. How will students sense that you care about them? Consider your personal mannerisms and whether students would perceive you as friendly, reserved, or withdrawn. What does your tone of voice convey? Your words and how they are delivered can encourage student listening and responses. When encouraged, students speak up; but sharp or abrupt tones can lead to disengagement in some students.

Creating a caring environment highly conducive to learning is more than great posters on the wall, desk arrangements, or fun activity centers. Developing the physical aspects, intellectual components, and relational community construct this environment. Keeping this environment takes maintenance and nurturing throughout the year; but at its foundation is respect. Give respect and you will gain it.

EpiPen®

This is a must-have device for students who are highly allergic to bees, peanuts, or other common substances. Per doctor recommendations, some students require an EpiPen® to be available at all times. Even if none of your students fall in that category, having one at hand is a wise precaution; so take it everywhere—playground, field trips, and emergency drills. Knowing how to administer an EpiPen® before you actually need to is best. You can learn from the school nurse or parent of the student needing the pen, or download information at www.epipen.com/how-to-use-epipen.

Exceptional Education Student Resource Time

No doubt you will have students who leave your room during the day to go to a special education room. To help these students remember when to leave and to avoid calling attention to their departure, give them a reminder clock. Tape a paper clock with their set departure time on the corner of the student's desk. A small battery-operated alarm or the student's own watch work well for older elementary students, because it allows more autonomy as the student sets and turns off the alarm.

Excitement

Students, especially elementary students, are easily excited by schedule changes, classroom visitors, and special events. To manage their excitement and expectations, let them know about these special activities ahead of time. Remember too that when students do get wound up, it's best to work with their energy, not against it. If students anticipate a special visitor later in the day, having them participate in a normal, quiet morning may be too much for them. Rather than trying to rein in their energy for quiet work, offer alternative activities that allow for their excitement. They can work in cooperative pairs or you might incorporate additional activities that use purposeful movement, such as responding to true/false questions about the day's lesson by sitting or standing. Channeling excitement into productivity is much easier than fighting against it.

Exercise

Students need movement. Research has indicated that the attention span of a two-year-old child is 5 minutes and approximately 20 minutes for elementary age children (Moyer & von Haller Gilmer, 1954). Lessons that incorporate movement or exercise are crucial to keeping students energized for learning. Adding movement to instruction does not necessarily mean reciting math facts while doing jumping jacks. Making a "game" of answering questions with simple movement seamlessly fits into instruction. For example:

> *Teacher*: "Listen to the following possible causes for the American Civil War. When you hear a true cause for the war, please stand. If you hear a statement that is not a cause, remain seated. When I do this [teacher makes sitting motion with arms], sit back down. I will say these statements once only, so listen carefully."

> "Everyone please stand. We are going to review the colors of the rainbow. When I say a color that is in the rainbow, please touch your toes. If I say a color that is not part of the rainbow, raise your hands over your head."

In addition to providing the healthy benefit of exercise, movement-incorporated instruction engages students, reviews critical information, and assesses student knowledge. From your teacher vantage point, you can observe which students respond immediately and which ones look to see what others are doing.

Expectations

Expectations not set can't be met! Clearly spell out what you expect in student conduct, and you minimize future poor behavior. Provide specific guidelines for behaviors before each cooperative learning lesson, class discussion, or trip through the school halls. Experienced teachers have seen firsthand how students live up to expectations. Also see **Preventative Measures**.

Expectation example

Teacher

Create a safe learning environment.

Treat each student as an individual.

Facilitate learning.

Provide frequent feedback.

Come prepared to teach.

Students

Come to school on time.

Come prepared to learn.

Treat others with respect.

Complete all assigned work.

Have a positive attitude.

Fairness

Fairness is not equivalence; it is not the same as identical treatment. Students may cry foul at a perceived inequity, yet your job in the learning process is to do what is best for each individual.

Achieving fairness takes awareness and considered action. Responding readily to students who are challenging is almost automatic and, in doing so, it's easy to forget about the attentive and quiet students. The fact that these students do not demand your attention does not mean they don't need it. "Good" students also need your time and energy.

When disciplining, you exhibit fairness by penalizing the few students causing a problem rather than dispensing a sweeping punishment. Being fair means keeping an open mind, not assuming, and giving opportunities to all students. Each child must be empowered to have a voice in the classroom. For example, don't assume that a naturally quiet student wouldn't do well giving a speech; some seemingly shy people shine in front of an audience. Also see **Justice**.

Though elementary students have a strong sense of fairness, they may need help in understanding it. The Character Counts (http://charactercounts.org) program by

Josephson Institute of Ethics has wonderful activities that help students understand fairness. Examples can be found at www.chiesman.org/action/charactercounts/pdf/FairnessPillarQuickies.pdf.

Field Trips

You can have fabulous field trips with preparation, planning, and perhaps a bit of creative resourcefulness. With limited school and classroom budgets, field trips may not be on your schedule the first year. If you find yourself in such a situation, set up a virtual field trip for your class. Field trips offer a look at the world outside the classroom, but both out-of-school field trips and virtual excursions require a lot of preparation.

Preparing for a field trip is certainly no walk in the park; careful planning and organization are crucial for a successful field trip. From required paperwork, permissions, and trip details to seeking chaperones, arranging travel, and keeping everyone together on the trip, field trips take time and attention to details. If you want to take students on a field trip not previously taken through the school, realize that you may need a year's advance notice to book your trip, depending on your site choice. See **Field Trip Checklist** in the **Extras** section.

Fights

Physical fights that go beyond the pushing and shoving that commonly occur among students may be rare in the elementary school, but they do happen. When a fight does break out, do not get in the middle of it. That is a sure way to get hurt! Placing a hand or other body part between two students may cause you to be bitten or hit. Use your voice to stop the fight: call the offenders by name and order them to stop.

One of the fastest ways to stop a fight is to remove the audience—the circle of onlookers. Often the students don't really want to enter the fight, but get encouragement from bystanders. Rather than lose face, they fight. If a fight breaks out, immediately send the bystanders to another classroom or call another teacher to remove them. Without an audience, the fight dispels, and you can deal with the fight's cause. To determine how the fight started, use the 5 Whats system. That is, phrase your questions so that every question begins with the word "what." Avoid phrasing any questions with "why," because it tends to bring about a defensive reaction.

Teacher: "What started this fight?"

Student: "He called my sister a name."

Teacher: "What about that caused you to get angry?"

Student: "My mom said no one picks on my family."

Teacher: "What would your mom think about you fighting in school?"

Student: "I don't know. I guess she wouldn't like it."

Teacher: "What could you have done instead?"

Student: "Told a teacher."

Teacher: "What will you do in the future?"

Student: "Tell a teacher."

First Day

Ready, set, action. There's no better time than the first day of school to roll out your management plan. Take time during the first part of the day for a class meeting to introduce it and discuss the following key points:

1. *Class rules.* Develop them with the students, phrasing each rule in a positive manner rather than creating a list of "don'ts." Remember to limit the number or rules and post them in a very visible space.
2. *Consequences.* Together with the students, identify consequences for broken rules.
3. *Classroom expectations.* Make sure you communicate your expectations regarding classroom culture, respect, and procedures.
4. *Procedures.* Introduce the main procedures for daily class operations such as morning routines, bathroom trips, pencil sharpening, dismissal, and specials.
5. *Rehearse.* Take time to practice the more complex procedures.

Parents on day one. Because it is the first day of school, parents may have special requests, including changes to their student's pick-up routine. They may want to pick up their child and a sibling or have a grandparent drive them home. It is extremely important that arrangements are made through the office or by whatever procedure your school has designated. Student safety takes precedence over parent requests. If your school does not require dismissal requests to go through the office, you may want to keep a form to track dismissal changes.

First-Day Fiasco

Prior planning and backup plans deter day-one disasters. To make the first day fantastic, try these helpful tips from a veteran teacher.

First-day readiness

- Prepare a newsletter for parents, introducing you and sharing information about the year ahead. See **Newsletters** and view a sample in **Extras**.
- Make multiple copies of your class and bus lists. Conveniently place them around the room. Copies by the door work as quick checks for fire drills and at dismissal. Also keep copies at your desk for attendance and other record-keeping purposes.
- Post class rules in a prominent spot in your room.
- Place the daily schedule, including special classes and events, and hang the lunch menu in an easily seen area.
- Place nametags on desks and in the books of younger students.
- Distribute books and supplies to the students' desks before their arrival. The time saved and the hassle avoided will be worth it.
- Create a chart noting the date of each student's birthday.
- Welcome students with preassembled gift bags containing pencils, stickers, an eraser, and a bookmark. Buying in bulk or from a discount store minimizes the cost.
- Plan a variety of activities that provide essential information and spark students' interest in the upcoming curriculum. Add more than enough to get you through the day.
- Read a special book or recite a quote to start the year positively.
- Determine carefully which classroom manipulatives and supplies you set out the first day. Keeping several in reserve lets you bring out fresh items later.
- Decorate a bulletin board or wall outside your classroom door to welcome students.
- Organize those numerous papers that must go home the first day in individual student folders or student-made envelopes.
- Give yourself a break if things don't go perfectly. Today is only the first day of many; you have tomorrow to do it better.

> —Marge James, 1st-Grade Teacher, East Stroudsburg
> School District, Pennsylvania

Focus on Problem, Not Student

When disciplining a student, focus on the problem, not the child. How you phrase a reprimand greatly influences its effectiveness and how it is perceived. Blaming the student only creates defensiveness or anger; but pointing out the behavior itself allows the student to find another behavior. Consider this example.

> *Teacher*: "You are the worst behaving student in this class. I don't know how you made it into this grade!"

> *Teacher*: "Your behavior is disturbing the other students. You must stop making those noises."

Food

When using food in the classroom, it is very important to be aware of three important things. First, consider the message you send if food is used as an extrinsic reward. Is food equated with success? Could an intrinsic reward replace an extrinsic reward? Second, check students' records for allergies or special diet requirements. You can look on the student health card or refer to a form that you provided to parents at the beginning of the year (see **Open House**). Third, be aware of school policies regarding food. Many schools have instituted a "bought goods only" policy for safety and health reasons. Also see **Rewarding Positive Behavior**.

Friending Students

Establishing good relationships with students is crucial to successful classroom management; however, it is not your responsibility to be a friend to students. Your relationship with all students must be professional. You can be friendly without being a best buddy. Show you care, listen, and give advice, but remain the professional adult. You can be personable and communicate that you care, but you must draw a line of demarcation between you as teacher and the students. Don't undermine your ability to exert authority. Once you cross the line, it's extremely difficult to step back to the other side.

Social media are places for that line. Friending students through social media is not a good idea for many reasons. You do not want your students to know everything about your personal life. Giving them access to these sites can very well offer them too much information. Your students may observe activities in your life and assume they can do the same things. They may not have the maturity to understand the difference between what is appropriate for adults versus children. Students also will share what they see with their friends and families, and your personal life may soon become the talk of the town. Even if you believe your posts are acceptable for a student audience, you cannot be sure all of your friends' posts will be. Besides, do you really want students to have 24/7 access to your life? You may end up resenting that nothing about your life is private.

Some teachers set up a teacher social media site for their students to discuss school-related topics. Whatever your personal opinion is on using social media sites, you need to follow your school's policies on this subject.

> *The value of rapport is possibly the most surprising aspect of behavior management I have found as an educator. It is vital to garner students' respect, not as a friend, but as their teacher.*
> —Maegan McCord, Learning Support
> K-2, Gilbertsville Elementary,
> Boyertown, PA

 # Gangs

Gang influence begins at a young age, and elementary school is not too early to be aware of possible gang involvement. Gang expert Michael Leonard (2012) identified characteristics that may indicate a child has ties to a gang, which are listed here and available at www. gangsrreal.com. Both teachers and parents should take action if an adolescent exhibits the following traits:

- Significant change in work habits
- Frequent absences from school (gang members skip school often)
- Changed vocabulary that includes a lot of slang
- New friends that may be questionable in character
- Sudden use of alcohol or drugs
- Behavioral changes or increased emotional mood swings

To help prevent children from being enticed by a gang, Leonard (2012) suggested parent involvement and proactive strategies. Teachers can enhance parents' efforts by applying these strategies in the classroom:

- Be an encourager.
- Help educate students about the dangers of gang membership.
- Do not permit any use of gang names, symbols, clothing, or graffiti.
- Monitor closely all computer activity to prevent students from online recruiting tactics.
- Treat students in self-esteem boosting ways so they won't be vulnerable to gangs.
- Encourage involvement in extracurricular activities.

Goodness

Sometime in your teaching career, perhaps even your first year, you will have students to whom you cannot relate or even find something to like. This can be especially true for students who have a history of negative behavior. Yet these are the very students who need a teacher's positive attention!

When you encounter such students, make an extra effort to look for goodness and offer praise, even if the good is something small. For example, if a "difficult student" happens to help another student stand up after falling on the playground or pick up a paper from the floor and give it to its owner, the effort should be noticed. This small act of helpfulness indicates a step in the right direction. Praise the student's actions (individually), without overdoing. You might say, "I was really proud of you for helping Jim up when he fell on the playground. You were being a good friend." What's more, when you search for goodness and praise it, you open your eyes to more goodness, and those praised are more prone to future acts of kindness.

Grade Book and Grades

The teacher's grade book is a legal document. As the legal record of a student's academic history, it can be summoned in court cases. Consistently recording accurate grades is vital. You should know that at the end of each academic year, most schools require teachers to submit their grade books, which are then stored at the school for a length of time required by the state—generally one to five years. During the next school year, you may or may not have access to that grade book.

Many schools require an electronic grading system, or you may create your own electronic records. If you develop your own, make sure that you *always* back up your computer and regularly run hard copies. You can find grading spreadsheets online through such sites as www.superteacherworksheets.com/excel-gradebook.html.

There are additional legal ramifications regarding grades. The Family Educational Rights and Privacy Act (FERPA) makes it illegal to publicize or post grades by student name or school number without first obtaining guardian/parent permission. Though this law applies to almost all areas of classroom grades, the Supreme Court ruled that it is not a FERPA violation to have students grade one another's papers: "Correcting a classmate's work can be as much a part of the assignment as taking the test itself. It is a way to teach material again in a new context, and it helps show students how to assist and respect fellow pupils. By explaining the answers to the class as the students correct the papers, the teacher not only reinforces the lesson but also discovers whether the students have understood the material and are ready to move on" (*Owasso Independent School District No. 1011 v. Falvo*, 2002). Teachers must be mindful that FERPA also applies to parent volunteers grading student papers. Only a parent who has a legitimate interest in the student should have access to another student's papers.

Grading

Like it or not, a good portion of your teaching life will be spent grading student work. Though time-consuming, it is an essential task for evaluating student progress. Using authentic assessments helps you make the most of your time and energy. Carefully select the tasks you collect for student grades, offer meaningful and helpful feedback on the finished assignments, and return them to students. Assessment strategies should match lesson goals and objectives; never assign busywork. Tasks must be meaningful; your time as well as your students' time is valuable. For evaluation and conferencing purposes, maintain accurate records on all student work and save samples of key assignments that showcase growth or concerns.

Grading Pens

What's in a color? Think back on homework returned to you and marked with the teacher's comments. What do you remember about his or her comments and the color of ink? Research conducted with teachers and students indicated that ink color influences how teachers grade and how students perceive their teachers (Dukes & Albanesi, 2012). Teachers tend to mark more critically when using red ink, and students associate negative connotations with comments and markings in red ink. With these studies in mind, consider using other colors when choosing grading pens.

Greetings

An effective way to establish a positive rapport with students is to greet each one at the door on a regular basis. A warm "Hello, how are you doing today?" or a handshake helps each student feel welcome and special. So that each student receives the greeting he or she is most comfortable with, you can place pictures of a high five, a handshake, a hug, and an X by the door. When entering the room, the student points to the preferred greeting. Many teachers find this method effective and it gives the student a feeling of control.

Whichever way you greet students, just doing so shows that you care and allows you to chat with them informally and get to know them a little more. Yes, this routine may reduce your time for any last-minute preparation, but it is time well spent. It is an investment in your students and a successful year.

Groups

When incorporated properly, student groups are wonderful, interactive learning communities. Through group interaction, students get to know and understand one another. Though there may be a few conflicts at first, as students work together, these conflicts become less frequent. To group students for lessons, games, and group projects, teachers can use both random and planned grouping techniques.

Random grouping produces the most spontaneous and interactive learning ensembles, but it usually works best when a task is not dependent on student ability. A nice element of random groups is that the students know the grouping is totally random, and the teacher needs only to point out that the grouping is temporary should a student complain about working with his or her paired student. New tasks bring new partners.

When a task or activity requires teams of either different or similar abilities, set up fixed groups. To form these groups, consider whether academic strengths are important or certain abilities. You many need groups for high, average, and low-achieving students, or ensure that each group has a good artist or mathematician.

 ## Grouping games

- **Animal antics.** Distribute index cards bearing the name of an animal, according to the group size desired. By making the sound of the animal on their card, students locate and group with the students making the same sound.
- **Candy mates.** Pass out a piece of candy to each student, having students group by candy type. As you can imagine, grouping by candy mates is popular with students, but be sure to consider allergy and diet concerns.
- **Famous couples.** Give each student an index card bearing the name of one half of a famous couple and instruct students to find the partner. Couples should be appropriate to students' ages and may range from historical figures to fictitious characters, for example, George and Martha Washington or Batman and Robin.
- **Musical matches.** Pair students by having them hum the song listed on their index cards. Choose widely known songs.
- **Penny pals.** Correlate the number of same-date pennies to the desired group size and form groups by pennies of the same late.
- **Old maids.** When pairing students, pick the number of desired pairs (24 cards, 12 pairs) and shuffle the deck of Old Maid cards in front of the students. Deal each student a card and let students find their pairs.
- **Suited pairs.** For larger groups, use a deck of cards to match students and designate roles within the group. For example, if you have 24 students and want groups of four, take out six cards of each suit (6 clubs, 6 hearts, 6 spades, and 6 diamonds) in 6 numbers (2, 3, 4, 5, 6, and 7) for a total of 24 cards. Shuffle the deck, deal the cards, and have students find their like number. You also can assign jobs within the groups by suit. For example, students holding hearts are materials managers; clubs, the recorders; diamond holders, the artists; and spade holders are the researchers.
- **Neighbors.** Sometimes simply turning to a nearby student works. Decide the direction to turn, pose a question, have students think about the

answer, and then give instructions with whom the students should share. This technique is commonly referred to as Think-Pair-Share (Lyman, 1981). Not only do students share their individual ideas, but they try to generate a better idea. Following the pair sharing, the pairs share their ideas with the whole class; ideas are usually recorded on the board or a sheet of paper.

Hand Signals

Save your voice and avoid interrupting classroom flow by using hand signals to obtain or reinforce appropriate behaviors. See **5 simple motions** under **Procedures Pave the Way**.

Health

See **Take Time to . . .** for teacher-related health matters and **Wellness** for information regarding student health records.

Help Desk

You don't have to be the only go-to source in your classroom; students can help one another. A student help desk provides a personal resource center that empowers students and frees you up to help students who particularly need your attention. When students are working independently, they can go to the help desk before asking you. The student of choice for the help desk depends on the project and ability required. Obviously, the helper student during math projects should be strong in math. Also, the student in charge should be able to explain directions and not just provide answers.

A less formal help desk is Ask Three, Then Me. This strategy works well when you need to work with a small group and have assigned seatwork. When a student is stuck or confused by the assignment, the rule is that he or she must ask three other students before seeking your assistance. Both a help desk and Ask Three, Then Me minimize disruptions when you must focus on specific students, groups, or projects.

Helpers

As self-sufficient as you may be, you will still want classroom helpers. The classroom is a community, and students need to be active and vital in that community. They can collect papers, clean up the room, tend plants, assist other students, and even help teach. Look for more ideas under **Student Jobs**.

You also can seek assistance from adult volunteers. After all, helpers in the classroom open up the doors of opportunities for both your students and you! From individual academic attention for struggling students to readying special projects or science experiments, classroom helpers give you more hands.

Though parents often are stretched many ways and may not be available as much as you would like or need, they are not your only source. Grandparents, extended family, high school and college students, and volunteers from community organizations often want to be involved in the schools but may not know where to begin. Show them! See **Volunteers** for detailed information about working with helpers in your classroom.

Helping Tools

Help comes in forms other than the human type. Ask any carpenter or designer—the right tools increase your efficiency on the job, ease the task at hand, and often even improve the project results. The following list highlights a few handy classroom tools.

- **Carpenter's belt or apron.** Project necessities are handy when you wear this tool-carrying accessory. Find one at a home improvement store and fill it with glue, markers, stickers, and materials appropriate to your current lesson or project.
- **Cat litter buckets.** Yes, you read that correctly! The plastic buckets that cat litter comes in make great mini libraries. With enough containers, books can be sorted by topic and buckets labeled accordingly.
- **Laundry baskets.** What works for laundry also works for Lost and Found boxes, playground equipment, and other oddly shaped items.
- **Milk jugs.** Quart milk jugs make great yarn holders. Cut off the bottom and thread the start of the yarn skein or ball through the pouring area. Yarn can be pulled without any rolling balls or tangled skeins. Multiple jugs are easily stored by threading a dowel through the jug handles.
- **Pill bottles.** Pharmacies will often give teachers unused pill bottles. They make great containers for small items such as beads and pins.
- **Skirt hangers.** Hang posters and large papers on skirt hangers that have clips. Clip the item to the hanger and place in a closet or on a rod.
- **Toolbox.** Toolboxes or plastic carriers help you lug various items in and out of school. Heavy-duty, plastic toolboxes are very durable and usually have a shelf, which is useful for small items. You also may want to purchase several inexpensive toolboxes for small-item storage in your classroom or closet.

Holidays

Just when students have settled into the routines and you are feeling more at ease with managing student behavior, along come the holidays! As much as you look forward to the festivities and vacation, students do too—doubly. They get wound up about a week before holidays and special events, becoming easily distracted and noisy, and exhibiting a new low in their motivation for schoolwork.

Wise teachers, which you must be, anticipate this pre-holiday mood and behavior change and plan particularly engaging lessons. They try to correlate lessons and homework to students' holiday or vacation activities and incorporate holiday-related and hands-on activities to interest students. Though class can't be all fun and games, the lessons and projects you plan for the weeks before the holidays must be especially appealing or you will not keep students' focus.

Before planning holiday–themed activities, however, you need to be aware of school policies and students who may be prohibited from engaging in holiday celebrations. Your mentor, principal, or another experienced faculty member can tell you about typical holiday celebrations within the school, including activities for nonpartici-pating students. Discussing these matters with the parents ahead of time helps you determine your options.

Homework

Organization. Designate a specific area where homework is placed each morning, such as one basket for math, one for science, etc. Teach students that their morn-ing routine includes placing homework in the proper baskets *before* the first bell rings. Also have a specific folder for homework that goes home: Tape closed the two short sides of an ordinary file folder and have each student decorate one. Work not completed during the day is put in the folder and taken home. At the end of the day, remind students to take home the folders *and* to put their finished homework back into the folder for return to school.

Policy. Who needs homework hassles? You don't and neither do your students or their parents. If you set clear expectations about homework from the first day of school, you will avoid homework headaches. Share your homework policy with students, parents, and your administrator. The policy should include an organized recording system, such as an assignment notebook or journal, and consequences for students who do not do an assignment.

Assignments. Help your students remember assignments by posting them regular-ly in the same places—on the board, class website, or school's homework hotline. Help them *finish* homework by giving them homework that reinforces concepts just learned and an estimated time that the assignment should take. Homework should not be new material that might prove overly difficult and frustrating to students and parents.

Hot Weather

Rising temperatures can easily lead to flaring tempers as students (and teachers) get overheated and crabby. Though you cannot control the weather, you can help control tempers. When you know the heat may be oppressive, plan activities that keep students calm and cool. Consider the following "cool" ideas:

- Read an interesting book to students. Being read aloud to is great for all ages.
- Play soothing music while students work on independent projects.
- Engage students in cool experiments. For example, a science lesson in which students make homemade ice cream and discuss freezing point depression offers hands-on experience and a chance to cool off on a hot, steamy afternoon.

Humor

Humor lessens tension, lightens the mood of the classroom, and lets students see your humanity (see **Be Human**). Laughter is good for the soul, as long as the humor is appropriate. It should never disrespect or ridicule people, especially students. Even if your friends don't laugh at your jokes, take a walk on the funny side with your students. They are a new audience. Establish a joke of the day, place a cartoon on a projection system at the start of class, or give students a chance to share their favorite jokes. Do set joke standards before your first comedian takes the stage.

Of course, humor isn't limited to jokes. Whim and wit can occur naturally during your interactions with students. Lightheartedness when all does not go as planned reduces anxiety and helps students enjoy their time with you.

Laugh it off ... and forward

Some incidents you just can't ignore, so you may as well address them with humor, as the director of a school play did during one embarrassing moment at practice. For her lead role, my daughter had to perform a special dance in a flowing dress. While twirling around during the dance scene, her dress raised high enough to reveal what was underneath. Immediately there was dead silence. She had neglected to put on the shorts she usually wore, so what was revealed was her thong underwear! The director simply stood up and calmly said, "And that's why we have dress rehearsals." Everyone laughed—including my daughter—and play practice moved on.

—Madeline Kovarik, Co-author, *The ABC's of Classroom Management*

61

Ignore Misbehavior

Ignore? Won't that create anarchy? No! In reality, you gain more by ignoring minor infractions rather than repeatedly confronting petty situations or annoyances. Pick your battles. Disciplining every infraction is virtually impossible—you would never get to teach. Neither do you want to become the nag whom students tune out.

Determine which behaviors most need to change, address them appropriately, and ignore less disruptive misbehaviors. Change doesn't happen automatically or immediately, so start small and work toward manageable goals. Also see **Baby Steps**.

What about the student who won't change behaviors, for whom nothing seems to help? Finding a solution that works is one of the biggest challenges teachers face when dealing with problem behavior. It often takes a great deal of time and effort. When a student is not moving toward cooperation or presents extremely aggressive or violent behavior, you must involve the parents and administration. Consider consulting a behavior specialist who can share positive behavior supports and develop a specific discipline plan for handling the most difficult behaviors.

Never give up on a child, but do recognize when a child may need specialized help or another placement. It's not your fault, nor have you failed, when you cannot solve all of the child's problems. Remember that challenging behaviors usually stem from complex situations that take time to resolve. For additional information on managing behaviors and discipline, see **Behavior Management** in the **Resources** section of **Extras** in this book.

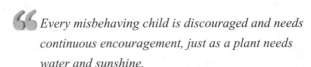

> *Every misbehaving child is discouraged and needs continuous encouragement, just as a plant needs water and sunshine.*
> —Rudolf Dreikurs, American Psychiatrist and Educator (1897–1972)

I-Messages

I-messages (Gordon, 2003) are a kinder, gentler means of approaching someone about unacceptable behavior, because they express feelings rather than confronting the person with judgmental or accusatory statements. When expressing I-messages, first state the problem in a nonjudgmental manner and then identify how the problem affects you; this usually includes your feelings about the problem. When these steps are accomplished, discuss possible solutions to the problem.

At first you may feel awkward using I-messages, but with practice you will feel more natural in delivering them. In turn, students change their responses to being called out on behaviors. Non-threatening I-messages are excellent communication aids because they help students—and adults—become aware of the effects of their behavior on others. By the way, do try this at home!

I-message examples

"Nick, I feel very annoyed when you speak at the same time I am. When you talk at the same time, neither one of us can be heard by anyone. I have to repeat myself and, consequently, we don't get our work done on time."

"I'd appreciate it if you would wait for me to call on you before you start talking. Then we can both be heard."

Inattentive Students

It can be aggravating, when students don't listen to your instruction or directives. You may begin thinking that your students are disrespectful. But wait! Things aren't always what they seem. Some students look inattentive, yet follow everything you say. Others try to listen but are preoccupied with personal or academic struggles. That students are distracted is not as important as getting them refocused.

Whatever reason students are sidetracked, get them back on task without being punitive. A simple way to gain a student's attention is to use his or her name in an example pertaining to the lesson: "James has a chicken that lays eggs every morning. If his chicken lays 12 eggs and James gives 6 to the neighbor, how many does he have left?" The first sentence brings James back to reality and gives him a chance to tune in to the actual math problem. Another solution is to use an activity to wake up the student. Ask an inattentive student to demonstrate what you are discussing, participate in a hands-on activity, or run an errand for you.

In-House Field Trip

This field trip is not for students; it's for you. Sometimes students get "under your skin," and despite your best efforts you are unable to get past your irritation. If only you had a break to regroup! When you reach this point, it's time for an in-house field trip. Before such an incident occurs, however, set up a "field trip" agreement with a neighboring teacher to send the student to his or her classroom with a "note." Per your agreement, when the student arrives with the note, the partner teacher delays a response to give you the break time you need. Remember that the trips must be previously agreed on and that students are sent only to supervised areas within the school boundary.

Is Fun Allowed?

"Start out strict and relax over time" was probably drilled into your head during your teacher training. Experienced teachers know that relaxing later is easier than reestablishing discipline, but does that mean you have to be all rules and no fun? Not according to Kriete (2003), who identified fun as a universal human need. She suggested that when fun is not constructively built into classroom practices, students resort to inappropriate ways to have fun.

Fun is vital to a cohesive classroom community. A fun learning environment motivates students internally (Erwin, 2003), and motivated students are more likely to work hard and behave appropriately. In addition, students are less likely to be stressed and more likely to feel a sense of belonging in an enjoyable environment.

Though school is not for entertainment, teachers should take advantage of fun learning. Games provide an engaging and enjoyable way to review information and prepare students for tests. Review for an upcoming science test with a round of *Bingo, Jeopardy!®,* or *Who Wants to Be a Millionaire?* With a focus on learning rather than competing, games energize students and reinforce facts and learning. Conducting lessons or reviews outdoors also invigorates students. Play kickball or softball to relieve test anxiety, reward jobs well done, and build community. Bust stress—have fun!

 *A class that plays together obeys together.*
—Anonymous

Jellyfish Teachers

Don't get stung by teachers and schools lacking structure, discipline, and backbone that Barbara Coloroso (in Charles, 2005) likened to the floating invertebrates that have little control over their destinations. Jellyfish teachers tend to manage inconsistently, failing to provide the structure needed for students to learn responsible behavior. They often drift on low expectations and extremes—swinging from lax rules to harsh and inappropriate measures when students get out of control. Set your feet on solid ground; don't be a jellyfish.

Journey

View each day of teaching as a journey. Think of your teaching as a long trip. Though the destination is a great distance down the road, you will encounter so many new experiences that half of the fun is getting there. With that in mind, be sure to make stops along the way, see the sights, experience what different places offer, and enjoy the ride. How important is the arrival when you didn't get anything out of the journey?

It's in your head

If you change your mind-set from summer countdown to daily appreciations, the atmosphere of your classroom will change. Students will observe that you value teachable moments more than just getting through the day to the last bell.

—Amy Dyer Moore, Lead Instructional Coach, Harshman
Magnet Middle School, Indianapolis, Indiana

Juggling Paperwork

One of the many responsibilities a teacher juggles is paperwork. Without a system, notes to parents, student work, individualized education program (IEP) reports, committee tasks, administrative data forms, and personal reports can become an out-of-control mountain of paperwork. One system for managing paperwork uses a calendar and folder to keep you on task.

On a calendar or plan book, write due dates in red. Back up ten days from the due date and write a reminder on the calendar in another color that is also different from the color used for plans or other events. Use these colors consistently to keep your "alert system" easily identifiable. In conjunction with your calendar, establish a to-do folder. As you get papers that require action, date the top right corner and place it within the folder in order of priority.

Each Thursday, check your calendar or plan book for due dates and events, using your color coding to help you recognize priorities. Looking at these items on Thursday helps you plan ahead for the upcoming week, alerting you to the tasks and projects you must finish. If you must push something to the week after that, you still have a few days to complete the task—though that specific job becomes a priority item.

Sometimes you may have multiple deadlines and conflicting priorities. When that happens, determine priorities and adjust your schedule. Keep in mind that your classroom priorities may come in second to administrative requests because school administrators often complete county reports using the data you provide. Not providing this information in a timely manner delays others as well and could negatively affect your annual teaching evaluation.

Prioritizing protocol

1. First ask yourself whether the task is something that *must* be done or something that you would *like* to do.
2. Is the paperwork needed for a meeting, such as an IEP conference?
3. Does someone else need the paperwork for a report or evaluation, such as an administrator completing a district report?
4. Is getting an extension possible?

Justice

Often justice is viewed as treating everyone the same. Classroom justice, however, has more to do with recognizing the individuality of students and interacting with them from that perspective. This characterization of justice is fundamental to successful classroom management because knowing what works for students individually is ultimately what works for the classroom. Some students need a little prodding, a few extra minutes, or a few more smiles throughout the day to do what is expected. Striving for across-the-board "fairness" only leads to frustration and stunted learning. Teaching and learning is far more valuable when the classroom atmosphere enhances individual potential. Also see **Fairness**.

Individual justice

At the start of the year, have students fill out a profile that asks them biographical information, such as nicknames, hobbies, fears, and favorite movie, book, and childhood memory. When profiles are completed, celebrate those "inequalities" that make each student exceptional—at that time and throughout the year. Justice, the kind students need, will emerge. You might hear the ring of justice when that child who needed the nudge thanks you at the end of the year for all the extra things you did just for her.

—Amy Dyer Moore, Lead Instructional Coach, Harshman
Magnet Middle School, Indianapolis, Indiana

Keeping Your Cool

Sometimes maintaining a calm, in-control-manner can be difficult, especially when misbehaviors are ongoing. Understanding central causes of misbehavior and when they're in force gives you knowledge and choices to help you keep your cool.

The main causes for misbehavior, according to Dreikurs et al. (2004) are attention, power/control, revenge, and helplessness/inadequacy, and they tend to occur sequentially. That is, if students do not get attention, they move to power. If that does not work, they go from power to revenge, and revenge to helplessness. If the cause is not obvious, you can reflect on your own feelings to help you identify the reason behind a student's misbehavior. If you feel annoyed or bothered, most likely the student is seeking attention. If you feel intimidated or challenged, the student's goal is power. If you feel hurt, the goal is revenge, and, if the emotion is the feeling of being incapable, then the student's goal is helplessness (Dreikurs et al., 2004).

Keeping your cool during behavior issues and working through their related emotions can be difficult. Journaling, seeking support through a teacher chat forum, and practicing de-stressing and management techniques help you deal with your feelings and provide perspective. Also see **Journaling**.

Keeping cool strategies

- Write out your emotions at the end of each day.
- Join a teacher group for support, ideas, and a safe place to vent.
- Count to ten.
- Take three deep breaths, s-l-o-w-l-y breathing in and out.
- Switch to a math activity (to shift the brain out of the emotional area).
- Send the student on an **In-House Field Trip**.
- Send the student or yourself on vacation.

Did vacation catch your eye? Though you may not be able to fly across the ocean, you can designate an escape space within your classroom, as one teacher did. Calling the time-out zone "vacation," this teacher outfitted a three-walled area with an Adirondack® chair, a sand egg timer, a bank, and a tape recorder with headphones. The walls were sheets painted with a beach scene, and the tape recorder was equipped with a recording of ocean waves pounding on the beach so that this "vacation" place was very inviting. When things got tough, students could self-select to go on vacation.

The trip cost them a chip, which was earned through completed homework and certain class activities. After depositing a chip in the bank, the student entered the area, put on the headphones, started the egg timer, and hit play on the recorder. During the three minutes of relaxing and regrouping, no one was allowed to bother the vacationer. Note that at first students overused vacation time, but once the novelty of it wore off, it was used only when really needed. Even the teacher visited this vacation spot, though without the headphones. She needed to hear the students around her, but it gave her the break she needed.

Kindness

Random acts of kindness among your students can cure interpersonal friction. It's amazing how having students perform spontaneous "niceties" for one another enhances the classroom atmosphere and reduces the number of management problems.

Random acts

Positive notes. Help students see the good in one another and themselves by having them write out positive traits. Supply students with a copy of the class roster. For each student, they write something positive so that everyone receives positive feedback. When the lists are completed, students anonymously submit the list to you. You then compile their lists of positive comments into lists for each student and distribute them. You also may want to keep a copy for yourself to add to the student's file and share during Student of the Week.

Typically, students are happily surprised at the wonderful comments made by their peers. This idea has been used for many years because it has been meaningful for many students, some of whom kept the list more than 15 years. In fact, when one student was killed in Vietnam, authorities found his positive trait list on him.

Secret sweetie. This award designation endorses kindness in the classroom and recognizes students who are exhibiting this characteristic. It's simple too. When you notice a student being kind, surprise him or her with a sweet treat and a brief thank-you note that are placed on the student's desk when he or she is out of the room. Note that awards like Secret Sweetie are most effective when students are unaware of possible rewards for their actions.

Coin jar. Encourage students to donate their extra change to the "coin jar." These random contributions then can be donated to a special cause voted on by the class.

Kinesthetic

Both beginning and experienced educators often avoid this learning style for fear of losing a lesson to chaos. Kinesthetic learners require movement, materials, emotion, and experimentation—all feared by those who struggle with classroom management. Yet, brain-based research has suggested that many students (especially inner-city, urban children) learn best with kinesthetic-styled lessons (Craig, 2003).

You can execute activities that promote movement and keep a measure of control by setting clear and concrete boundaries. State your expectations and accept nothing less.

Kinesthetic language arts

1. Group students in threes or fours.
2. Supply one small beach ball per group.
3. Write instructional commands, such as "describe," "analyze," and "compare," in the colored sections of the beach ball.
4. Have students toss the ball to one another. When the ball is caught, the student must answer according to the instructional word facing him or her regarding the current unit being studied.

This method stimulates students' ability to remember and process information. Though kinesthetic learning activities may mean more movement among students and most likely an increase in the noise level, they are worth offering on a regular basis. There is no reason to fear activity in the classroom—wonderful learning often happens in a noisy atmosphere. Also see **Noise in the Classroom**.

Laugh

Laugh when you do something stupid and when a student does something funny. Smile. Be silly. Laugh. Don't be afraid to use humor in the classroom—as long as it is not sarcasm. Two of the most powerful stimulants for memory retention are novelty and emotion. Linking lessons to emotions, particularly humor, helps cement learning. Think about a wonderful day in your life. Chances are that you remember the emotions more than the facts. Let laughter into your learning atmosphere; it's good for building better relationships and there's nothing like a good, hearty laugh to relieve tension. We've all heard that it takes more muscles to smile than to frown, so use up those calories and laugh (then you can justify that extra piece of chocolate!).

Library

Classroom libraries can be expensive to create, but there are several options for building one without major damage to your budget. Look for books at yard or library sales, making sure to read through your choices to ensure they are appropriate to your grade level and school's media guidelines. Another option is to set up a Books Offer Student's Success (BOSS) program, as a Florida elementary school did to help its teachers build their classroom libraries. Ask parents to donate old books that their children have outgrown. Once books arrive, a small group of teacher volunteers meets after school to review books for content and determine an approximate reading level. The school's first–year teachers receive a bundle of books for their classroom library as a welcoming gift. Parents benefit too because they clear space on their children's bookshelves, knowing that other children can enjoy the books.

Location, Location, Location

It's everything in real estate and, believe it or not, in successful classroom management. Where you are in the classroom is important. Optimize your location in the classroom: circulate, circulate, circulate. Too many teachers cling to the front of the classroom, rarely moving about the room as they teach. When you move about the classroom, you become aware of all areas of the classroom. Not only does your location help you keep tabs on students' academic progress and behavior, but it encourages those students who are reluctant to ask questions in front of the class to seek your assistance.

Lockers

If your students store coats and books in lockers, allow time on the first day to practice opening and closing their lockers. Working a combination lock the first few times and getting to class on time with the proper materials are challenges that make students anxious. A little extra time at the beginning of the year to get used to a new procedure results in smoother transitions in the long run. Also see **Transitions**.

Lounge

The teachers' lounge can be a positive or a negative place. What you say in this area and how you handle what you hear determine which it is. Be careful about what you share. Remember that you are a professional who is expected to be confidential regarding your students. For example, perhaps one of your students tells you that his parents had a big fight the previous night. Later in the teachers' lounge, a colleague who does not have this child in class says to you: "I heard there was a big row at the Mitchell's last night and the police were called. Did Johnny say anything?" How do you respond? The best answer is, "Sorry I don't know anything."

Love Teaching

Many teachers entered the profession because they love children or because they felt called to the field. For many, teaching is a calling, not a job. Whether you can say that about yourself at this stage of your career, start your professional journey by finding those things about teaching you love. Develop your passion for teaching. Passion for what you do cements your commitment, lifts you above the mundane, and inspires you as a professional.

Be proud of your professional status! Hang your diploma in your classroom, just as doctors and lawyers do in their offices. After all, you *are* the expert when it comes to learning and student achievement. Be proud of who you are and what you do. Teaching is important, but hard work. Think about it this way: there are 24 hours in a day. If an elementary student sleeps 10 (don't we wish they all would get that much?), that leaves 14 hours. Approximately half of that (6½ hours in the school day plus time getting to and from school) is spent with you. If you ever think that you are not having a profound influence on your students, remember that they interact with you as much (and in some cases more) than they interact with their families. Be proud. Be passionate. Love teaching!

> *Teachers should understand that teaching is not a job, but a calling. To motivate* [teachers]*, it is important that they are strengthened to be passionate towards teaching. It is very important for every teacher to understand that professional self-development in teaching skills is highly important. Feedback is a vital part of teacher motivation. Everyone wants acknowledgment that they are doing a good job, and suggestions on how they can do even better.*
> —Grace Pinto, Managing Director of Ryan International Group of Institutions, Mumbai, India (Rao, 2010)

Love Your Students

Gordon (2007) described the benefits of loving the people you associate with in any type of setting such as schools and places of business. He suggested that this outpouring of love enhances a group's enthusiasm, productivity, and performance. But what does that love look like and how can you show love to your students? These suggestions may help you love your students:

- Spend time with your students.
- Learn about them as persons—ask about their hobbies and interests beyond the classroom.
- Take the time to talk with and listen to your students.
- Recognize their efforts and successes.
- Make an effort to bring out the best in each student.

Lunch Count

Early in the school year, take pictures of your students and glue the pictures on magnets or put students' names on Popsicle sticks. When students enter the classroom in the morning, each moves his or her magnet or stick from "home" to one of three columns: school lunch, home lunch, extras (e.g., buying ice cream, milk). Immediately following morning announcements, a student helper counts the number in each column and writes the name of any absent student. The teacher can quickly scan the room to make certain the student is truly absent. This method saves time when submitting lunch and attendance counts. When lining up for lunch, the teacher then can call students by the column groups. With each group lined up in order, students get through the cafeteria line quickly. Also see **Attendance**.

Lying

Your students must know that lying is not tolerated in your classroom. You, however, need to realize that lying is somewhat common among children, especially when they are caught doing something wrong. Introduce your policy on lying by reminding students that the classroom is a place for respecting one another and that lying is one of the worst forms of disrespect.

How you respond to a student who has lied depends on the age of the student and the severity of the situation. It is helpful to first try to determine the reason or cause of the lying. Did the child lie to get attention, to cover up an error and avoid punishment, or was there another reason? You can discuss the situation with the student and then, once you have a better idea about the reason, you can take disciplinary measures appropriate to the age of the child.

For most children, the denial of a privilege may be appropriate. In some situations, a warning might be appropriate—especially if this is the first time this misbehavior occurred. It will be important to help students understand the importance of being honest, as well as the consequences and problems caused by lying.

Keep in mind that proving that a student is lying is difficult; however, many students "fess up" when direct eye contact is used during a discussion of the problem. Older students who have mastered the art of lying may never admit guilt. Such situations require discernment and careful decision making on your part based on the evidence available. When students do admit to lying, acknowledge and praise them for being honest and having the courage to come forward.

> *Living up to basic, ethical standards in the classroom—discipline, tolerance, honesty—is one of the most important ways children learn to function in society at-large.*
> —Eloise Salholz, former Senior Writer at *Newsweek* magazine

Manipulatives

Managing mathematics manipulatives and their use can be a problem. As with other materials, clearly explain to students how you expect them to distribute, use, and collect the manipulatives, and be consistent in these expectations. Be sure to give students time to become familiar with new manipulatives before giving a specific assignment. Designate the areas where they are to be used and how many people can work together. You also may want to assign roles (e.g., Leader, Recorder, and Custodian) when students work in groups to ensure learning time goes smoothly and manipulatives are returned to their storage area.

Storage of manipulatives definitely calls for organization and consistent management. Match the size of manipulatives to containers and use clear shoe boxes for many objects. They stack neatly and contents are easy to see. Other handy and effective (though perhaps a little unusual) storage containers include:

- Spice racks—for small items
- Flower pots—inexpensive metal ones are colorful and easy to label
- Frosting containers—work well for rolled up items such as measuring tapes
- Self-closing plastic bags—can be hung by a bent paperclip on a tension curtain rod

Managing columns of numbers

Are students having difficulties aligning columns of numbers for accurate calculations? Use graph paper with large boxes. Free downloads are available online or you can purchase paper. In a pinch students can turn a wide-ruled notebook paper sideways so that the lines define the columns. This makeshift graph paper is great for calculating decimals.

Meetings—Faculty

Required faculty meetings vary by school, but you can be sure you will attend them. It may seem to be a waste of precious time you could use for lesson planning or grading, but they are important in several ways. Even as your mind begins to scroll through your classroom things-to-do list, pay attention. Keep informed. Besides, your active participation shows courtesy to the presenters and exhibits professionalism to your colleagues.

No matter how good you are at multitasking, the faculty meeting is not the place to grade papers or file your nails—as a former colleague once did. Listen, nod your head in agreement, and be prepared to volunteer. You are likely to be asked to lead a project or participate on a certain committee. When this happens, remember to set limits. Your priority in the first year is to perfect your teaching skills. Opt for short projects that will not impact your entire school year. Should you need to miss a meeting or leave early, notify your school administrator ahead of time so that he or she is aware of the reasons. The most effective classroom manager shows respect, whether a leader or participant.

Mentors

The first year of teaching is stressful because you are not only learning the curriculum, student needs, and systems within the school (i.e., who to go to for what) while developing relationships with parents, but you also are learning to be a good teacher. Learning to teach is like learning to ride a bike; at first you have to concentrate on so many tasks that you do not really enjoy the ride. Yet you keep working at mastering cycling until, after a while, the ride becomes easier and you enjoy yourself more.

Fortunately, in teaching, you do not have to wait until the end of your first-year ride to find ways to "make the ride easier." Mentors can help, and having one during this first year is important. The school may assign you a mentor as part of a formal orientation program, or you may choose someone on your own (informally). Though it may be hard to open up to your mentor about difficulties, know that your mentor truly is there to help and that a mentor does not influence your administrative evaluation. Your mentor is your guide on your first-year journey. Cultivate the relationship and know that someday you may be the mentor. You also can connect with mentors outside your school through Kappa Delta Pi's Teacher Hotline and State Teachers of the Year via the KDP website and at conferences. These master educators are valuable resources.

Model Appropriate Behavior

When your students do not behave appropriately, you must show them the behaviors you expect from them. Whether or not they "should have learned this at home," the reality is that you want actions in your classroom different from what they exhibit. It's up to you to teach and model your expectations.

Students need to understand the difference between formal and casual behavior and when those behavior types are appropriate. Formal behavior is practiced at work, school, religious services, and other organized group situations. Casual behavior is most typically used with friends or at home. Your students enter school well versed in casual behavior, but they have not fully learned or even understand the importance of formal behavior. Children who do not regularly participate in situations requiring formal behavior may not have learned necessary skills. Yet knowledge and use of formal behavior is crucial to a student's success in the school environment. As the classroom leader, it becomes your responsibility to teach and model appropriate behavior.

Acting out specific scenarios and explaining the reasons behind your modeled behaviors introduces students to appropriate formal behaviors. Role-play a scene where you are carrying a large stack of art supplies and a student accidently bumps into you, knocking the supplies to the floor. As you pick up the items, you say to the student, "When you accidently bumped into me, all the things I was carrying fell. Would you please help me pick them up?"

To help bring home the point, you then can explain to the class that you had many choices of responses when bumped. Mention that you could have pushed the person back, sworn, or yelled at the person for not paying attention. Emphasize that your response of using appropriate words is the "school way" to handle such incidents.

When children have not learned appropriate actions, they do not know to respond accordingly. Yet these situational behaviors are essential for entering the work force. Teacher leaders model these behaviors and explain both appropriate and inappropriate behaviors for situations. Also see **Best Practices** and **Cursing**.

Model Humility

Just as modeling appropriate behaviors is important, so is modeling humility. After all, no one is perfect. Perhaps you become impatient with a student or respond with more sarcasm than humor. Show students you accept responsibility for your actions. When you blow it—and you will—model humility and express regret for your behavior. Apologizing reminds your students that you are human. It also demonstrates accountability and respects those involved. Modeling humility speaks volumes to your students.

Motivating the Unmotivated

Intrinsic motivation is the ideal way to learn or change behaviors, but sometimes it is not enough. Then what? You may have to do a little detective work. Observe and talk with the unmotivated student to discover his or her interests outside of school. Learn about special hobbies, favorite sports, television shows, and games that he or she enjoys.

Once you know interests of the unmotivated student, you can reward his or her positive behavior with an activity related to one of those interests. You might, for example, play the student's favorite game to reward positive behavior or acknowledge genuine effort. In addition to encouraging more positive behavior, participating in a favored activity helps create a bond with the student.

> *I have thought about it a great deal, and the more I think, the more certain I am that obedience is the gateway through which knowledge, yes, and love, too, enter the mind of the child.*
> —Anne Sullivan, Teacher and Companion of Helen Keller (1866–1936)

Music to Manage By

Music is a powerful classroom tool—in learning, managing, and creating atmosphere. Even if you have never played an instrument or you are tone deaf, you can incorporate music in your classroom.

Learning. Lessons put to song imprint on the brain in a unique manner. As Routier (2003) stated, "Music's physical vibrations, organized patterns, engaging rhythms, and subtle vibrations interact with the mind and body in many ways, naturally altering the brain in a manner that one-dimensional rote learning cannot" (p. 8). Think of the songs you can still sing though you haven't heard them for years. What if lessons stuck in students' brains as well as those commercial jingles you wish you would not remember? That's the power of music!

You may have learned your multiplication tables or state capitals to a song. Draw on your own experiences and visit online sources, such as www.songdrops.com, for music that teaches.

Behavior management. In *The Role of Music in Classroom Management* (2003), Jackson and Joyce discussed the positive influence of music on classroom behavior. Routier (2003) called this impact the "Mozart Effect," stating that when listening to Mozart's music, there is "improvement in concentration and speech abilities" (p. 8). Children who receive regular musical instruction tend to be more advanced in reading and language skills.

Music also can manage the mood of the classroom. It calms, soothes, and relaxes. When students are wound up from physical education class or recess, playing soft rock, smooth jazz, or classical compositions can help them settle down. Conversely, when students are restless and off task, having them dance to faster-paced, rhythmic songs releases their pent-up energy so they can regain focus.

> *Musick has Charms to sooth a savage Breast,*
> *To soften Rocks, or bend a knotted Oak.*
> —William Congreve, English Playwright,
> in *The Mourning Bride* (1670–1729)

Lyrics manage too. Don't overlook the powerful effect of song lyrics as a management tool either. Meaningful lyrics give insights, encourage compassion and empathy, and promote class discussion. Kick off a lesson about teasing and cruelty, for example, by playing country singer Mark Will's "Don't Laugh at Me." Talking about what the song means and how it feels to be made fun of gives insight to those who may not realize how their words and actions affect others.

When choosing music for your classroom, do make sure it is age appropriate and that lyrics adhere to school policies. Music played during assignments should be instrumental only; many students could be distracted by singing.

Transition cue. Music also can signal transitions. Songs, poems, and finger plays help younger children transition from one activity to another. A designated passage of music or a stroke across a small xylophone can indicate that it's time to clean up, go to lunch, have story time, or prepare for dismissal. Monitor group activities by playing background music. If the music can't be heard, the noise level is too loud.

Names on the Board—Not!

Since the beginning of school classrooms, teachers have written students' names on the board when they misbehave as a reminder of the offense and its consequence. But how effective is this procedure?

Students who misbehave tend to have self-esteem problems already. Consequently, advertising a misbehavior may harm more than it helps. Some students are humiliated, while others feed on the negative attention. Neither outcome is healthy or motivating. Why not privately list students who have misbehaved? You can keep accurate records, yet respect privacy.

New Students

When students come into your classroom later in the year, they do not always arrive at the beginning of the day, because registration usually takes a significant amount of time to complete. You may not know in advance about a new student, so try to have books and first-day items ready in case of a new arrival. When you do know ahead of time, have a desk and set of textbooks ready. You also might assign both a male and female student (for restroom reasons) as Class Ambassadors, who meet the new student when he or she arrives. The role of class ambassador not only is welcoming to the new class resident, but also gives the ambassador experience in hospitality etiquette.

The ambassador helps the new student adjust to the class by showing where things are located, being a friend, and introducing others in the class. During their five-day role, ambassadors sit with the new student at lunch and escort him or her to the restroom if needed.

When determining seating, place him or her behind other students for the best assimilation. Though it seems special to place someone new at the front of the room, sitting behind others allows the new student to observe others and learn classroom procedures. See **Open House** for a new-student introduction idea.

Newsletters

Classroom newsletters are an important form of home–school communications that need to go out on a regular basis. Though a weekly newsletter is preferable, its frequency depends on time constraints and whether students can assist in the newsletter's production. Assess your teaching load, and set a weekly, biweekly, or monthly schedule. Then follow it. Parents need to know when to expect a newsletter. Send home the initial newsletter the first day of school. Introduce yourself, perhaps include your picture, and give an outline of classroom expectations and plans for the year ahead.

Keep the newsletter's format consistent to help parents readily find important information, such as dates to remember and your contact information. Take time to double-check your newsletter for spelling and grammar to ensure it is error-free. For sample newsletters, see **Resources** and *ABC's Online*.

What's in a newsletter?

- Date of newsletter.
- This Week We Study. This column lets parent know current units and lessons.
- Things Our Classroom Needs. Keep your classroom stocked by sharing its needs in a regular column. List project needs, from paper towel tubes to volunteers, along with the dates items are needed.
- Thank You to . . . . This column offers a note of appreciation to people who contributed to the classroom. List their names and contributions.
- Dates to Remember. Remind parents of school pictures, the next test, and other need-to-know-activities.
- Congratulations to . . . . This column is a great place to recognize students for accomplishments outside of school, such as an earned belt in karate or a Little League team win.

No Complaining Rule

According to Gordon (2008), a "No complaining rule" helps develop a positive environment in your classroom. He suggested three practical ways to lessen the amount of complaining:

1. Turn a negative statement into a positive one by adding the word "but" followed by a positive statement or action. Challenge student complaints with that format. For example: "I don't like math drills, **but** I know they help me learn my math facts."

2. Change the phrase "have to" into "get to" and attitudes change too. Encourage a positive focus: "We **have to** read to the first graders once a week" becomes "We **get to** read to the first graders once a week."

3. Direct complaints to solutions. Help students find a remedy for their complaint. For example: "There's nothing to do outside at recess!" can be a prompt to ask the physical education teacher about borrowing balls and jump ropes for recess or to request a PTA fundraiser for playground equipment.

> *You don't make progress by standing on the sidelines, whimpering and complaining, you make progress by implementing ideas.*
> —Shirley Chisolm, first black U.S. congresswoman (1924–2005)

Noise in the Classroom

When does noise become noisy? How do you keep the purr of students working together from building to a distracting roar? You may find it difficult to determine how much noise in a classroom is appropriate. Many novice teachers do. Though your school environment often dictates what a suitable noise level is, a rule of thumb is whether the hum of your classroom distracts nearby students or teachers.

As for your personal preference, noise becomes noisy when you feel that the students are getting out of control. Only you can determine that. It's very important, especially during your first year, that your classroom functions at a level in which you feel in control.

Turn down the volume!

Develop a signal that lets students know to get quiet immediately. Introduce and practice it the first week of school. The type of signal you choose doesn't matter, only that everyone in the class knows what it means. Suggestions for signals include:

- Raise a hand or an index finger.
- Turn off the lights briefly, when safe to do so.
- Clap a rhythm.
- Ring a bell.
- Call out a catch phrase such as "give me five" (students respond to five raised fingers).
- Change the stop light. On a cardboard traffic light, indicate noise levels with a large paper clip or arrow. An appropriate noise level gets a green light. As the noise level increases, move the clip to yellow and help students notice the change by standing at the light for one minute. Do not speak; simply stand there. When the noise level decreases, move the light back to green, thank the students, and remind them to keep their voices down. If the noise does not decrease, move the indicator to red and signal for whole class attention (see **Whole Class Attention**). The class then must remain totally quiet for one minute after which you remind them to lower their voices and return the clip to green.

Does all noise bother you? If you find that you prefer silence most of the time, you need a reality check! Children are social creatures. Expect noise during group work and projects. Sharing knowledge and ideas is inherent in the process of learning. Ensuring that students stay on task while conversing is your challenge.

Noise that Bothers a Student

Some students are more sensitive to noise than others. If one is distracted by noise, allow that student to wear headphones. Check the school for a broken pair and cut off the wire. Earmuffs work too. In case of an emergency, however, the student should still have some hearing capability.

Non-Procedural Questions

Questions for which an answer is not truly intended are non-procedural questions. Such questions are ineffective and can even cause a classroom behavior problem.

When you ask, "Is everybody ready?" as a signal to students that it's time to leave for lunch, you invite feedback. Though you meant the question to be a rhetorical prompt with no response expected, the fact that it's a question leaves it open.

More effective to classroom management is stating a command rather than asking a non-procedural question. Tell the class when to be ready to leave for lunch or PE class: "Everybody needs to be ready by the time I count to 5. Raise your hand if you do not understand." If students need more time, give them a three- or five-minute warning. Another form of the non-procedural question is "Okay?" Often it serves as a sentence filler between thoughts, though you may be unaware how often you say it. Check yourself by videotaping a lesson. Because you do not really seek students' permission for most classroom procedures and instruction, eliminate "Okay?" from your vocabulary.

Notes about Student Progress

Sometimes you need to note a student's progress or document when a problem is indicated. Such notes are essential when it comes to assessing academic or behavioral progress, communicating with parents, and keeping you in tune with a student's needs. An easy way to take these notes and compile them is to use a note folder. Simply tape 5 × 7" index cards in a stair-step fashion on one side of the folder, and then place the students' names alphabetically on the steps. When you see something noteworthy, jot it down on the card with the day's date. This note file helps you maintain formative assessment information all in one place. It also allows you to quickly scan cards to determine whether the same problem is occurring in many students, in which case you need to reteach the concepts.

Notes Home

Personal notes home are valuable. They open up communication between home and school, keep parents informed on student progress, and show parents or guardians that you care about their child. Handwritten notes personalize the information, showing that you took time for a special communication. Keep your notes professional in appearance and without spelling and grammatical errors.

Setting up a system for notes home ensures that every family receives a message. To ensure that every student received one note home in a month, designate 7 or so students, depending on the size of your class, to receive a note. In the notes, discuss positive work or progress by the student: "Raj has worked so hard this month on his multiplication table. He now knows 1–7 by heart. I am so proud of the progress he is making." Or "Today, Sam was in an altercation on the playground. Instead of getting in a fight, he chose to use appropriate words to solve the problem. He really made a good choice today. I am proud of him." These note should share only complimentary information and avoid any reference to future improvement or past difficulty ("I wish Sam would do this every day," or "I hope Raj will do as well on the 8 and 9 times tables"). Simply focus on the praise.

Before sending the note, make the student aware of its content. Many children only get parent contact when they have done something incorrectly. If you want to be sure parents receive the note, postal mail is preferred. By sending home positive notes, the students are praised for appropriate action. Parents and students alike take pride in these positives notes.

Notes to Students

Sticky notes are a great way to share comments and praise with a student. If you notice that a typically off-task student is focused on work, just write a sticky note such as "Love the way you are working on this paper!" and casually stick it on the corner of his or her desk. These little reinforcements help to modify behavior because you are giving praise to the student for doing the right thing. These short and sweet notes work especially well for the attention-seeking student.

Observations

By administrators. Administrators like to complete two types of observations: *formative* and *summative*. A *formative* observation is typically a "walk-through" by an administrator. Good administrators get out of their office and walk through the building at least once a day, dropping in on a few classrooms. Many administrators practice what is known as a 5-by-5 rule: they walk through all classrooms in the building, but observe for 5 minutes only in 5 selected classrooms. During such observations, they may take notes on a handheld device.

Observations keep the administrator aware of overall school and classroom climate and informed on specific teachers and their practices. They allow an administrator to document teaching activities helpful to completing a teacher's annual evaluation.

A summative observation is a formal classroom observation, which usually entails a 20–30-minute visit. You are likely to be asked to suggest several dates and times for a formal observation and, during observation, you can expect the administrator to take copious notes. These notes, combined with the formative evaluation notes, make up the teacher's annual evaluation that usually occurs well after the observations.

By peers. Most school districts offer a new teacher mentor program that pairs an experienced teacher with a new teacher to support and guide the novice educator during this critical year of teaching. Mentor observations and subsequent feedback usually are components of such a program. You also may request an observation by a colleague you believe is an excellent professional.

Think of observations and evaluations as learning experiences, and listen to feedback with an open mind. Though you may have worked at having the "perfect" lesson, realize that an observer can see what you cannot. Accept comments or critique without defensiveness, asking questions to make sure you clearly understand what is mentioned. Remember, learning continues throughout life and comes in many forms—from coursework, peers, mentors, and even students! Being observed by colleagues is so helpful that it is well worth reaching out to a peer for constructive feedback even when you have a mentor.

By self. You may be your worst critic, but you also can be your best observer. You already know lessons that have gone well and those that have not. You probably know your weaker areas of practice and when you feel most confident, but you can enhance this knowledge by videotaping yourself. Filming yourself several times a year lets you see your improvements and catch habits of which you are completely unaware, such as calling on the left side of the room more times than the right side. Seeing yourself in action can prompt changes that never may have occurred to you without a video.

> *I once videotaped myself teaching in what was at the time a favorite dress of bright yellow. After watching the video, I never wore that dress again. I looked like Big Bird! What was I thinking?*
> —Madeline Kovarik, Co-author, *The ABC's of Classroom Management*

Office Referrals

Sending students to the front office for discipline should be reserved for particularly serious behavioral offenses. Whatever the reason for the trip, you also send an unspoken message to both the student and the administrator. To the administrator it says that you have classroom management issues you cannot control. To the student it says, "I can't control you." Do not relinquish your power.

After all, the front office does not have magic dust that fixes a student. Suspension is the one solution the administration dispenses that you cannot—and that resolution ultimately is not in the best interest of the child. Seek creative management techniques and work to know and understand a difficult student. Don't give up on a student and don't give up your power.

One Size Does Not Fit All

No single style works every time when it comes to classroom management. If you teach more than one group of students, don't be surprised when a strategy that works like magic with one class bombs with another. Not all students respond alike. Effective classroom management is a work in progress—a plan tweaked and honed during the year and throughout your career. Be open to adjusting your approach for different types of students, and don't give up on the first try. Plan ahead, but realize that trial and error often become your greatest teachers.

Open House

Your school's Open House, Back-to-School Night, or Meet the Teacher Night is your "debut" with parents. It may be parents' first impression of you (and perhaps you of them), and it is the perfect opportunity to cultivate a working partnership with your students' families. For some beginning teachers, this meeting is a little nerve-racking. Even experienced educators can get nervous when it comes to making that first impression or speaking to a group of adults.

One such teacher was "Emily." She was great with students and even loved to "ham it up" with them, but she froze when it came to being in front of a group of parents. Open House was a nightmare for her. A creative problem-solver, she came up with an innovative solution. Rather than speaking at Open House herself, she videotaped the students talking about life in her classroom and what parents could expect throughout the year. Each student had a role in the video, which excited students and parents alike. At Open House, she welcomed parents and then showed the video. Imagine the parents' delight as they saw their own children! Ever resourceful, this terrific teacher saved the video so that she could send a copy home, along with a welcome letter, to families of a new student.

What to share at Open House

- Daily schedule
- Curriculum and testing
- Homework policy
- Grading
- Classroom rules
- Special events during the year
- Home–school communication (let parents know how to contact you and when, notes and newsletters they'll receive, and how to inform the school and you on schedule changes for dismissals)
- School policy on divorce/separation paperwork regarding custody (see **Custody**)

Open House is not just to inform parents. It's also an excellent time to enlist parent involvement and gather additional information about students, such as food allergies. Let parents sign up for activities, helping in the classroom, or working on projects at home via a volunteer sheet that lists possibilities. For more about this list and getting parents involved, see **Volunteers**.

Realize that you cannot cover every topic or answer every question at this meeting. Speak briefly, direct parents' questions to topics relevant to the entire group, and prepare a classroom newsletter or FAQ sheet to help parents remember key items.

Organization

Entire books and websites are devoted to getting organized. They exist because organization of plans, materials, and time leads to successful management of your day, whether you're a first–year teacher or a veteran. When you don't plan well, too much time and energy is lost on daily tasks. Alleviate problems before they start by building your management plan on a foundation of organization.

Daily tasks

- Prepare all lesson handouts, manipulatives, and materials before class, placing them where they are easily accessible during instruction.
- Put up a morning assignment for students to begin shortly after entering the classroom.
- Post the day's schedule to give students a heads-up on the day's activities and include an inspirational quote or cartoon to establish the classroom mood.
- Jot down observations about individual students throughout the day to add to their records later.
- Assign set routines to students.

Long-standing tasks

- Establish an efficient procedure for collecting and distributing papers and supplies. It may be a set routine or student-assigned task (see **Student Jobs**); it just needs to be orderly enough to become routine.
- Designate a drop-off zone for homework and a pick-up place for important papers, such as centrally located "In" and "Out" baskets.
- Create individual student mailboxes for the delivery of important papers.
- Use take-home folders for homework and papers, especially for younger students (also see **Homework**).
- Create individual student files for work samples, important notes, papers, observations, and other student documentation. Log and date each representative item as well as any communication to and from parents and administrators regarding the student.
- Develop an attendance monitoring system. Calling out names lets you greet students individually, while having them sign in allows you to focus on other tasks.

Materials

- **Daily handouts.** Make a filing system with compartments for each day of the week in which you place all copies to be used on a particular day in its corresponding compartment. By checking your plans at least three days ahead of time, you allow yourself enough time to get copies made.
- **Supplies.** At the end of each month, inventory your classroom supplies to ensure adequate materials for the next month. Maintain a list of both ordered and used supplies from the beginning of the year.

- **IEP papers.** Students who have special needs have individualized education plans (IEPs) that guide their instructional abilities and needs and must be documented as goals are accomplished. Keeping paperwork current is vital (see **Juggling Paperwork** and **Record keeping**). Update these files weekly, if not daily. Be consistent; it is far easier than playing catch-up. Note: Store the confidential IEP files in a locked place.

- **Unit materials.** Store together all materials related to a particular unit of study. Once you finish the rain forest unit, for example, place the bulletin board items, artifacts, sample projects, and associated literature in a clearly labeled container. Include an inventory sheet of the contents. The next time you teach the unit, you'll have what you need. You can always add or refresh contents, but you won't have to start over or spend an excessive amount of time searching for materials.

Classroom Arrangement. As you arrange your classroom, ensure that you have a line of sight to all areas. Semi-private areas for students are great, but students still must be visible to you. If a bookcase divider wall blocks your view when you are working with students at the reading table, it also blocks efficient classroom management. Test your arrangement to make certain you can see everywhere in the room, wherever you are.

Great arrangement

One effective room design organizes desks into table groups of four, with an inexpensive shelving unit on wheels at the end of each group that serves as a resource center. The top shelf can house a can of extra pencils, tray of rulers, box of tissues, mini-sized trash can, and a handheld pencil sharpener. On the next shelf are tubs or bins containing materials for the current lesson that can be slid on and off the shelf when needed. Books and materials needed only occasionally get placed on the bottom shelf, which frees up space in students' desks. This arrangement keeps materials close to students, which minimizes classroom disturbances. Students can help maintain this arrangement by taking on jobs such as emptying the trash can, sharpening the pencils, and straightening the shelves before dismissal.

If desks in rows work best for your classroom, you can help students keep the rows straight by placing a sticker (dot or square) where the right leg of the desk should align. When leaving for lunch or at the end of the day, have students "check the dots" to get desks back in line.

Outcasts

Sadly, almost every class has at least one outcast or social misfit who just isn't accepted by other students. All too often, this student becomes the source of jokes, mocking, and mistreatment. It is up to you to help students realize that such behavior is not tolerated in your classroom. When an incident with this student occurs, take immediate action—looking the other way only increases problems.

It is also up to you to recognize your own predispositions. As much as you may love children, you will have students with whom you have difficultly connecting, or who have irritating behaviors, odors, or personality traits. That is normal; you are human. Such situations, however, call for you to examine your own attitude before discussing your students' behaviors toward the "social misfit." How do you treat that child? What do you communicate verbally and nonverbally? Remember, children are incredibly perceptive, easily picking up on your feelings about particular students.

In addition to monitoring behaviors toward the "outcast," you can help the student be viewed more positively. Point out a unique talent, skill, or trait that will help the child be respected. Accentuate the positive and minimize the negative to help other students see this student in a more positive light. Showcase a special talent or ability, or ask a well-liked student to show respect for this student as an example for others to follow. You also can consult the school guidance counselor for suggestions and assistance.

> *He drew a circle that shut me out—*
> *Heretic, rebel, a thing to flout.*
> *But Love and I had the wit to win:*
> *We drew a circle that took him in.*
>   —Edwin Markham, American Principal
>   and Poet (1852–1940)

Page Numbers

When identifying page numbers during a lesson, give the page number orally and visually. Say it aloud and write it on the board or hold up a textbook turned to the appropriate page. Despite the repetition, you are likely to have at least one student ask, "What page?" When that happens, do not respond. Instead, simply point to the number on the board. Students will stop asking and start looking.

Parents

Establishing a good rapport with your students' families may take extra effort but is crucial to a good working relationship with them, which leads to academic success for the student. Developing that relationship happens at several levels, from an initial phone call telling parents something positive about their child to creating activities to involve families in the school community. Here's a look at various aspects of the "parent factor" in the classroom.

Two-way communication. Open the windows of communication by letting parents know how and when to reach you. Do not leave it open-ended; it only leads to misunderstandings and frustrations. By taking the lead and designating your availability, expectations are clarified. Only you can decide when parent-initiated communications should occur. Though some teachers share their home or cell numbers with parents and make themselves available after school, many administrators encourage teachers to reserve their evenings and weekends for family and recharging time.

When setting time frames, tell parents when you are available for phone calls during the school day and when they can anticipate replies to emails. Explain that you are unable to answer phone calls or emails outside of these times because your responsibility is to your students. Changes in dismissal or emergency situations should have their own procedure. Ask parents to alert you to the content of the message in the email's subject line. For more information about communicating with parents, see **Relationship Building**.

Unexpected arrivals. What should you do when a parent pops in to talk just as students are arriving for the day? Unless it is urgent, politely let the parent know that your job is to focus on students' arrival, as it sets the tone for the day, and that your foremost responsibility is to the students. Ask the parent to please contact you by phone during your planning time so that you can give your attention to the discussion. Sometimes parents are concerned they will not be able to reach you or they just do not realize how disruptive a "quick conversation" can be at that hour.

Parents as partners. Working in conjunction with parents brings about greater student success than working independently from or opposed to them. When dealing with behavioral issues, parents are your best allies. They know their child the best and may be able to shed light on the reason for a child's misbehavior. Perhaps a recent event triggered the problem.

To get this working relationship off to a good start, contact parents *before* any problem arises. Let them know through a phone call or note home what you appreciate about having their student in class. Make sure parents are informed about your classroom happenings, including your behavioral management plan. Tell them at the start of the school year so that there are no surprises, should an incident occur.

When a problem does arise, share your concern with parents. Whether the issue is academic or behavioral, addressing the situation immediately and informing them through progress reports keeps them in the loop regarding their child at school. Remember to retain records and copies of your communications—notes, phone calls, emails, and meetings. Records are important for many reasons: follow-up, tracking, evaluation, and back-up.

To further promote parents as partners, you can offer special activities that feature an aspect of the curriculum, either in conjunction with other team members or for your classroom, and invite students' families. One popular event is Family Science Night, where students and their families come to school for an evening of hands-on science activities. Read about setting up this event in the **Extras** section of this book.

Conversing with parents about a problem. Guillaume (2004) recommended using a warm, supportive tone when talking with parents to let them know you care about their child and want to help. Both what you say and how you say it reflect your level of care. Speak in a positive, authoritative manner, without coming across condescendingly. When discussing a difficulty, try "sandwiching" the information. That is, begin the conversation with positive statements about the student's attributes and successes, followed by a frank explanation of the concerns you have about their child's behavior or academic progress. End the conversation with another positive comment.

Crucial to expressing care is addressing the behavior, not the person (Guillaume, 2004). You are seeking parents' assistance in resolving a behavior problem, not fixing a problem child. State your concerns in factual statements, backed by documented examples of misbehaviors or academic struggles, avoiding comments that imply fault or trigger defensiveness from the parents.

During this conversation, give parents time to share their insights. Learn what works for them and seek their suggestions or questions. Be sure you really listen to their responses, even if they are not exactly what you had hoped to hear. Sometimes parents react in the moment and need more time to consider the situation. Reassure them that together you can help the student, and then develop an action plan with them that deals with the problem.

For the best implementation of a plan, outline specific steps or actions for each of you to take. Close the conversation with a clear plan for working together to solve the problem and give a copy of this plan to the parents. Restate positive comments about the student and work together so that parents leave hopeful about an effective resolution. This plan and supporting documentation should be placed in the student's file.

If parents become angry or exhibit threatening behavior, end the meeting. Suggest meeting again later, when a professional conversation can occur. At that meeting, you need to have another professional present for your support and safety, such as the principal or guidance counselor. You do not need to remain in a situation where you feel endangered or are not treated like a professional. Besides, nothing can be accomplished in such a meeting.

Parents as volunteers. When parents volunteer in the classroom, they not only contribute to their child's education, but witness their child's in-class behavior. If they have not volunteered previously, they gain an awareness of what takes place in the school. To learn more about parent helpers, see **Volunteers**.

Parents from other cultures. Most schools have students who are from a culture other than American. Many times, their parents are non-English speaking, which may limit school–home communication. In such cases, take steps to encourage involvement. Though communicating with parents from other cultures may pose a challenge, the cultural richness they bring to the classroom is a gift to be cherished. Invite them to share their culture with the class.

Communicating with non-English speakers

- Request help from the school's ESL teacher.
- Have the child translate if he or she is English speaking.
- Determine whether other families in the school share that culture and enlist their help to translate communications.
- Request a translator for IEP meetings.
- Seek local community college or university students who are from the culture or studying the language of these families to request translation help.
- Check for translation software programs available through the school.

Parent-Teacher Conferences

Your first parent-teacher conferences may seem a little intimidating, but if you prepare thoroughly and brush up on communication skills, you can confidently and successfully conduct them. Plan for your conference by considering which important information needs to be shared with the parents and how you will do it. Show parents examples and related documentation that back your concerns.

Just as in other meetings about a student's behavior, good conferences first discuss the student's positive traits and accomplishments, followed by concerns focused on behavior or performance, not the student's character. The conference is then closed with additional positive statements and an optimistic outlook (see the tip, **The conference cookie**).

If you believe that the behavior issues may require outside assistance, such as educational testing or evaluation by a medical doctor or psychologist, you only may suggest this to parents. It is not your job to prescribe a next step, only to offer possibilities in helping the student progress.

Again, retain a written record of the conference that is dated and signed by all attendees and provide a copy for the parent. Not only is this record important for backup and student evaluations, but also is necessary when a student is referred for school counseling or child study teams.

The conference cookie

Layer one: "Jayden is such a wonderful young man. He gets along with others in the class and is liked by everyone."

Filling: "Jayden, however, has a hard time distinguishing when it is okay to talk and work with others and when he should be paying attention to the lesson. This is influencing his grades, as you can see in this progress report."

Last layer: "I believe Jayden can change his behavior and do well this semester. He is a bright young man and has the ability to be successful."

Patience

Often touted as a virtue, patience is a necessity when it comes to classroom management. Even veteran teachers struggle from time to time, so don't beat yourself up if you wrestle with managing your classroom. Be patient—with your students and with yourself.

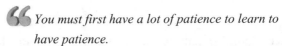

> *You must first have a lot of patience to learn to have patience.*
> —Stanislaw J. Lec, Poet and Aphorist
> (1909–1966)

Pencil Sharpening

Having a student get up to sharpen a pencil during a lesson is annoying, especially when the trip to the sharpener has more to do with an "in-house field trip" than a dull pencil point (see **Attention**). You can have a rule of no pencil sharpening during lessons or, if you don't mind movement while you are teaching, you can have a pencil exchange cup where an unsharpened pencil is exchanged for a sharpened one. At the end of each day, one student sharpens those in the cup so they are ready for the next day. For related information, also see **Procedures Pave the Way** and **Student Jobs**.

Photos

Before you post photographs of your student on the class website or publish them in the school newsletter, get consent from the family. Most schools use a release form that allows photos and the student's name to be released to the media. This form must be kept on file. If your school does not have a form, you can create your own. A sample form is available in the **Extras** section of this book and at *ABC's Online*. If a parent refuses to sign the form, it is your responsibility to ensure that student does not appear in any published photos or articles.

Playground Preparedness Bag

Lots of things besides play can happen on the playground—including injuries, emergencies, and discipline referrals. To be prepared for incidents and accidents, create a playground basket or bag to hold various emergency kit items, such as a water bottle (for rinsing a cut), bandages (for minor scrapes), office discipline referrals (in case of a fist fight), clinic passes (for the nurse's office), a pad and pencil for notes, and an emergency form. When you take students to the playground, also take along your cell phone to gain prompt assistance in case of an accident. One item not to include is medication. You should not apply medication on a student following an injury as a precaution against an allergic reaction.

Positives vs. Negatives

Most individuals respond better to positive reinforcement than negative reinforcement. When developing a set of rules for your classroom, focus on the positive. Display "do's" rather than a list of "don'ts." For example, instead of the rule "No yelling," use the phrase "Use inside voices in the classroom." When a misbehavior occurs, encourage behavior change by referring to students who exhibit the behavior you expect: "I really like the way Sean's group is working together on their assigned poster." This approach compliments appropriate behavior and sends a message to other students that they need to do that as well.

Poster Power

Have you noticed how your students tend to look toward the ceiling when trying to recall an event or answer? That is because they are trying to create a mental image of whatever it is that they are trying to recall. You can capitalize on this natural tendency and enhance recall by orderly arranging curriculum materials around your room. Keep math, language arts, social studies, and science materials in their given area throughout the year. This established pattern helps students know where to look for certain information and empowers their recall. When testing situations require posters to be covered or removed, you will find that students look at the blank wall to visualize the poster.

Power Struggles

Power struggles with students are, at best, no-win situations. Avoid them! When a student taunts you, either verbally or nonverbally, with the message "You can't make me," do not try. Avoid getting drawn into proving it—because you really can't.

Though the human response to threatened authority is to fight back, doing so is the surest way to lose authority. Check your first reaction and then respond calmly. You are the professional. If a student refuses to sit down after being asked, debating the issue—especially in front of the class—will get you nowhere. Instead, firmly tell the student that he can choose to sit down now or see you after class. It may seem as though you are surrendering to his wishes by delaying action; however, holding out leads to a later victory (see **Defiant Students**). When a student is particularly disruptive, have him or her accompany you into the hallway for a controlled, but firm, discussion.

Power whisper

Speak softly (and carry no stick) to get a student under control. Standing close to a student and speaking softly, so that only the student can hear, effectively brings about better behavior.

Practice

Practice, practice, practice is what teachers often tell students: Practice free throws and playing the recorder. Practice multiplication tables and practice spelling words. Practice because practice makes perfect, right?

Not necessarily. Something practiced incorrectly does not lead to the intended learning or accomplished task. Monitoring these tasks refines practice, which supports success. In other words, "only perfect practice makes perfect."

Praise

The best praise teachers and parents can give students is that which is specific to a task or accomplishment. It is easy to throw out a phrase such as "good job" or "that's correct." These words are meant to encourage similar endeavors in the future; however, they do not really tell a student exactly what he or she did to achieve the praised success. Effective praise mentions what the student did to earn the comment. Acknowledge the student's hard work in finishing a project or the practice time he or she spent to finally ace a math fact test. Of all the classroom management techniques teachers can employ, praise is the most immediate and likely yields the greatest results.

When a student answers a question correctly, you can provide effective praise not only by affirming that the response is correct, but also by indicating why. For example, "You are correct. The sun is a star." Doing so affirms the answer and reiterates the correct information for the class. You also can amplify a student response when praising: "You are correct. The sun is a star. In fact, it is the closest star to the earth." Amplification increases the student's knowledge and augments the lesson.

Preventative Measures

As you plan lessons and activities, anticipate potential snags in your plans and prepare for those as well. For example, if you know that Josh and Kayla tend to bicker with each other, avoid placing them in the same group. If you have been forewarned about a possible fire drill "sometime next week," take advantage of that knowledge and build flexibility in to your schedule, especially if your lessons include a science experiment or test.

> *An ounce of prevention is worth a pound of cure.*
> —Henry de Bracton, English Jurist and
> Writer (ca. 1210–1268)

Principles for Dealing with Principals

What should you communicate to your administrator, and when do you have the discussion? How do you know when to send a child to the principal? Your first and foremost guide is your school's policy, so refer to and rely on it. When a major policy is violated, notify the principal or other appropriate administrator. Severe problems, such as violent behavior, threats, serious bus issues, and weapon-related concerns, always must be reported immediately. For a difficult issue not outlined in the school handbook, consult your mentor or another trusted colleague. Also see **Office Referrals**.

Otherwise, managing classroom behaviors is in your hands. Maintaining control of your class on your own builds your confidence and displays your competence to students, administration, and colleagues. When a student's poor behavior continues, collaborate with the parents before involving the principal. They know their child best and can share strategies they have found helpful. If parents are unresponsive, or they place the responsibility entirely on you, immediately talk with your principal.

Communication between you and your principal is not only about behavior issues. Principals want to know teachers and their relationships with students. They like to hear about special projects and community efforts. Cultivate an open and professional rapport with your administrator. The following principles can help.

More positive principles

- Keep the principal informed on your classroom—share both good news and challenges. Send the principal a copy of your classroom newsletter or notes to parents that talk about the exciting classroom you have created.
- Tell the principal about any significant problems with a student or parent. Principals need a heads-up on potential crises and do not like to be caught off guard.
- Invite the principal to special events in your classroom.
- Be forthright and prepared if you are questioned by the principal about a practice or classroom behavior. Know your rationale for that practice.
- When presenting a problem to your principal, also provide suggested solutions. It shows that you have given the situation serious thought and are working toward resolution. Rather than dumping a situation, you essentially are seeking approval or alternative suggestions for the situation.
- Mind your manners. Never speak ill of your principal—not with parents, colleagues, or students. Avoid complaints in the teachers' lounge. It is totally unprofessional, and nothing good comes of such conversations.

—Pam Kramer Ertel, Co-author, *The ABC's of Classroom Management*

Prioritizing

Many well-organized teachers who comfortably juggle various responsibilities still find themselves struggling to keep up with paperwork, lesson planning, and messages via voice mail and email. Should you find yourself overwhelmed with messages, IEP reports, papers to grade, and faculty memos, revisit your priorities.

Planned priorities

- After picking up your mail, separate out the junk mail as you return to your classroom.
- Sort your mail next to the garbage can or recycling bin. Toss junk mail, unopened, into this file-13 receptacle.
- Throw out mail that you viewed but don't need to address.
- Separate the remaining mail into three baskets: Immediate Attention, Do This Week, and File.
- Check and sort emails at a designated time daily. Delete junk mail and respond immediately to as many emails as you can.
- Place messages to be addressed later into a file marked as such.

Problem Solving 101

Solving problems isn't your job alone. Students can and need to learn how to seek positive resolutions to problems. Don't expect that they already have the skills to do so, though. No matter what age your students are, start with basic skills in conflict resolution, guiding them and practicing techniques until they understand.

Syllabus for problem solving 101

1. Identify the problem. Allow individuals involved to share their feelings and needs about the situation.
2. Brainstorm possible solutions to the problem.
3. Evaluate solutions individually using the question, "What would happen if?"
4. Select what is thought to be the best solution and try it.
5. Monitor that solution; continue using it or seek a new one.

Procedures Pave the Way

Procedures or routines are the first line of classroom management, outlining expected student behaviors for specific activities in the classroom. They are the foundation of classroom management on which you develop additional management plans and build a cooperative community.

When you establish routine procedures for student movement, topical or class transitions, non-instructional tasks, materials management, and group work, behavior management is built into your classroom. The keys to making these procedures effective are to establish clear-cut routines, put them in place on day one, and practice them again and again. Practice, practice, practice!

When introducing a procedure, be sure to let students know what the exact consequence is for not following the procedure. Practice the routine immediately after introducing it. Time spent in practice is worth it in the long run. Further reinforce a procedure by having students verbally reiterate each step involved.

Common procedures

Arrival and dismissal routines. If you love chaos, then don't plan these routines! If, however, you prefer an orderly beginning to the school day and a relatively smooth student exodus, establish specific procedures. On arrival, children must quickly put away their coats and books, turn in homework, and prepare for the day ahead. A posted assignment settles students into the classroom while deterring off-task socializing. You may wish to reinforce this routine and reward prompt accomplishment with student choice reading time.

Dismissals usually are the most chaotic. Therefore, the first rule to implement is that you—not the bell—must dismiss students. When the bell rings, students want to charge out the door. If it's been a tough day, you also might welcome such an exit. Mad dashes, however, mean forgotten homework, backpacks, mittens, or even coats. Set up orderly routines for gathering books, projects, papers to go home, and personal items. Stick to those routines, and you and the students will go home happier.

Fire drills. Follow your school's policy for fire drills, but prepare students for what they must do and where they should go in case of an emergency. Periodically walk through these procedures to instill in students what they need to do if an emergency occurs. Always keep a class roster by the door to help you account for all students during drills and emergencies.

Materials management. Established procedures for distributing, collecting, and storing instructional materials allow students to complete these tasks easily, efficiently, and autonomously.

Other non-instructional tasks. Plan procedures that let students help you take attendance, collect permission slips, do participation counts, and keep the classroom neat.

Restroom and water fountain breaks. Your school may have a policy but, if not, determine the best procedure for your students: a whole-class bathroom break or one student at a time. See **Bathroom Breaks** for several possible procedures.

Transitions. Help students transition smoothly to the next lesson or activity by setting up self-directed materials and instructions. One technique is to list items needed on the daily schedule.

5 simple motions

Hand signals are great nonverbal directional procedures. They work well because students are told or reminded verbally, visually, and kinesthetically—and kinesthetic reinforcement of expectations is especially effective with elementary children. Additionally, simple hand motions allow direction or correction without interrupting instruction or pointing out a particular student. A poster of these procedures, accompanied by pictures of students doing the corresponding motions, helps remind students of these signals, further reducing the need for a verbal reminder.

1. *Follow directions.* Extend your pointer finger straight up into the air and make a circular motion.
2. *Listen.* Show two fingers, then make an L shape with your thumb and pointer finger, and put it up to your ear.
3. *Raise your hand.* Show three fingers and raise your hand above your head.
4. *Keep your hands and feet to yourself.* Show four fingers, shake hands, point to feet, and cross arms.
5. *Never hurt anyone on the inside or the outside.* Show five fingers and then shake your head while pointing to your heart and out toward the students.

   —Erika Lee, Kindergarten Teacher, Aurora Public Schools, Aurora, Colorado

Professional Attire

If you want to be treated like a professional, dress like one. Always wear clothing that is neat and appropriate for your position. Modest apparel is appropriate. Teachers often lean over to help students at their desks, pick up items off the floor, and retrieve books from low shelves. Think about that when choosing a top to match your skirt or slacks. Tops should cover your midriff and necklines should not expose cleavage.

Also appropriate are the right shoes. Sensible shoes are a must! Learn from the new kindergarten teacher who wore stiletto heels the first day of school. After being on the move with her students all day, she never wore them again.

Sensible shoes also do not include flip-flops. They may feel comfortable, but they are not professional attire. Their flip-flop sound is distracting, and they are not considered safe shoes for many work environments. Dress professionally and appropriate to the teaching position you hold.

Project-Based Learning (PBL)

Taking a constructivist approach to classroom instruction changes your role and the classroom environment itself. Along those lines, project-based learning engages students in working together toward a common goal in problem solving or project completion. In project-based learning curricula, you are a facilitator of learning more than an instructor, helping students develop their ideas and gather materials necessary to complete their projects.

With the collaborative nature of PBL, you can expect more noise and movement than in other forms of instruction and perhaps some conflict among students working together. This too is expected and part of the learning experience. It even can be a growth opportunity. Well-planned PBL units, though, actually can minimize classroom management problems, because students enjoy working together and being engaged in hands-on activities. As the facilitator, you guide the collaborators and their work to make sure these interactions are appropriate, safe, and productive. For suggestions on minimizing conflicts and handling management concerns, see **Groups** and **Noise in the Classroom.**

Propinquity

There is power in propinquity—being nearby. You can deal with a disruptive student without interrupting the flow of a lesson simply by moving closer to him or her. Try it. The next time you see a student playing with something in his desk or passing a note to a neighbor, simply move closer to the student. Your closeness increases the level of concern and, most times, the disruption stops.

Proximity

Nearness is not always about curbing off-task behaviors. How close we stand or sit when conversing with others is related to our cultural experience. Not all cultures have the same norms regarding body space and proximity. Americans tend to prefer more personal body space than other cultures. Recognizing this difference in cultures is important when relating to students and parents from cultures different from yours. If you feel uncomfortable when someone enters your personal space, simply explain that it makes you feel uncomfortable and that you need a little more space. On the other hand, if you tend to move in closely to someone when conversing, you may find that some people step back. If so, it may be that they are uncomfortable with that proximity and would relate better with more distance between the two of you.

Proximity control

Placing easily distracted students near you helps them work more productively. Proximity also allows you to monitor individual progress. When circulating about the classroom, frequently stop by students who are easily sidetracked or needy. Your physical presence deters misbehavior. If an incident arises, you can readily handle it privately.

Questions

With the right questioning, you not only receive answers, but also engage learners and stimulate higher-order thinking. Furthermore, when students are focused on lessons, they are less likely to need management. Teachers' questions done well are keys to good teaching.

Additionally, when students ask the right questions, they learn how to become well-informed lifelong learners. Teacher-generated questions fall into four categories: managerial, rhetorical, closed, and open.

- *Managerial* questions keep the lesson moving (e.g., "Is everybody focused on me?").
- *Rhetorical* questions reinforce an important idea or concept (e.g., "Thumbs-up or thumbs-down: Was slavery the only issue in the Civil War?"). Also see **Student Reponses**.
- *Closed* questions check mastery (e.g., "How much is 8×7?").
- *Open* questions stimulate discussion (e.g., "Why do you think Alice went down the rabbit hole?").

These questioning techniques target higher- and lower-order thinking responses, both of which should be part of classroom instruction, because each helps students acquire and retain knowledge. Higher-order thinking uses analysis, synthesis, and evaluation (Bloom, Engelhart, Furst, Hill, & Krathwohl, 1956). Lower-order questions ask students to recall facts, while tapping knowledge, comprehension, and application. To ensure that your instructional questioning is balanced, you can create index cards of prompts to reference during lessons. Examples of such prompts are available at *ABC's Online*.

When asking questions, pause before calling on a specific person. Doing so causes the entire class to think of the answer, because no one knows who may be asked to respond.

- *Teacher*: "Jerome, can you name an animal that is a carnivore?" (Only Jerome has to pay attention to the question and think of an answer.)
- *Teacher*: "Can you name an animal that is a carnivore? [Pause] Jerome?" (Your pause lets all students consider the answer, just in case you called their name.)

Quick-Access Spreadsheet

Information on students is critical, as is easily retrieving it. A spreadsheet containing the following information is important to have on hand for emergency situations:

- Student name
- Parent name (it may differ from the student's)
- Address

- Phone numbers (home and mobile)
- Referrals to exceptional education programs
- Enrollment in exceptional education programs
- Grade retentions
- State test data (e.g., language arts, math)

Most of this information can be obtained from the student's registration form or yearly cumulative record. Keep the spreadsheet current and retain copies of it at school and home, because you never know when an emergency situation might occur.

For example, a kindergarten teacher received a phone call at home from her principal about the death of one of her students. During the call, the principal mentioned that she had arranged for the school guidance counselor to discuss the concept of death with her class. The teacher realized she needed to make parents aware because some might prefer to discuss matters with their child themselves. Having her spreadsheet at home allowed her to contact them right away.

Quick-and-Easy Attention Grabbers

With a room full of students, getting everyone's attention on short notice can be difficult. That's why teachers use quick attention grabbers to quiet students immediately. To ensure the success of your attention grabber, teach its meaning and the expected response to it when given. For silent attention grabbers, see **5 simple motions** under **Procedures Pave the Way**.

Your attention please!

- Turn off the lights.
- Clap a rhythm.
- Hold one hand in the air.
- Ring a bell.
- Say "freeze."
- Develop an acronym or phrase that means to stop and listen, such as SALAME: **S**top **A**nd **L**ook **A**t **ME** (Wong & Wong, 2005).
- Say "All eyes on me."
- Play a short musical passage—sound three notes or stroke a xylophone. See **Music to Manage By** for more ideas about managing the classroom with music.

Raising Hands

By fifth grade, it seems that students would have learned to raise their hands in class. Ask any 5th-grade teacher, however, and you will hear that they have not. Regardless of the grade level, students must be taught the act of raising hands to speak in class. You can train them to raise their hands—without "ohhh, ohhhh, ohhhhs" and foot stamps—simply by not calling on or acknowledging them and, instead, calling on the student whose hand is raised properly. When naming that student, state why he or she is being chosen: "Thank you, Troy, for raising your hand quietly. What was one of the causes of the fight between the Hydra and Hercules?" Do not call on or acknowledge someone who is acting inappropriately so that you do not reinforce the inappropriate behavior.

Reality Check

If you are not yet convinced of the extremely public nature of social media sites such as Facebook, Twitter, Pinterest, and Google+, think about your answers to the following questions regarding recent posts on your favorite sites.

- Would you want your students to have access to photos taken on your spring break in Cancun?
- Would you want the hiring superintendent to see photos of you and your friends at your graduation celebrations?
- Would you want the parents of your students reading your posts and friends' replies about how you spent your weekend?

Yes, you have the right to free speech and you can "live your own life," but the reality is that you are part of a community and, in your position, you influence part of that community—its children and their parents. If you want that community, as well as your colleagues and administrators, to respect you as a professional, you must carefully consider how you use social media. If you decide to keep a page on Facebook or another site, make your presence professionally acceptable by following these guidelines:

1. Do not post intimate messages between you and your significant other.
2. Post only pictures that are acceptable for all to see, especially your students.
3. Refrain from posting any pictures or messages that refer to your consumption of alcohol.

4. Do not post pictures or text information that presents you in a negative light. Remember, data is forever.

5. Pause before posting. Think about who might see images and content and how easily they are found on the Internet. Google that!

6. Accept your responsibility as a professional and role model. Realize that your students are highly influenced by your behavior, so much so that your posts can influence them, whether or not your messages were intended for them.

Recess

If your school is among those districts still providing recess, make the most of it! Recess is a great time for students to get exercise and expend pent-up energy. Of course, when all that energy lets loose, recess also can become a "great" time for tempers to flare and arguments to escalate. To head off problems during recess, get students active in organized play. They are less likely to stir up arguments when games with rules guide their playground freedom. Other preventative measures include:

- Supply activity-based, portable equipment, such as balls of various shapes and sizes, jump ropes, Hula Hoops, beanbags, and sidewalk chalk.
- Circulate during recess to interact informally with students and check on their interactions with one another.
- Serve as a referee during games to help provide an objective view and keep tempers in check.
- Develop a procedure for getting students' attention in order to quickly exit the playground and return to the classroom.

It is important to remember that recess is for your students, not you. Though it is tempting to talk with your peers at that time, your job is to keep students safe by constantly circulating and observing. It is your responsibility to monitor your class at all times. For more recess related information, also see **Playground Preparedness Bag**.

Record Keeping

A teacher entered the officer of her principal, threw herself down in a chair, and said: "Nobody told me that teaching had so much paper!" With the requirements for IEPs, ESOL, SLD, and 504, you may say the same thing. Many new teachers can feel a little overwhelmed by the abundance of forms, notes, and files they must generate (also see **Juggling Paperwork**). Though much paperwork is required, especially in cases of students with special needs, this record keeping is important and its accuracy critical for many reasons. In addition to showing student progress, these records detail academic needs for assistive tools, referrals, and other resources. Beyond the students' needs, these records are required documentation for school funding requests.

If your school does not have established and expected procedures for setting up and maintaining records, consider this process. Review the student's Individual Educational Plan (IEP), behavior contract, or English as a Second Language (ESOL/ESL) plan to determine required modifications. In your plan book, document *each time* you make a modification for the student. You may want to keep a list of possible modifications in the student file so that you can log the date on the prepared list, adding new modifications as needed. Modifications on your list could include the following items:

1. Extra time on tests (T) and assignments (A)
2. Quiet testing environment (QT)
3. Reduced homework/in-class assignments (RA)
4. Preferential seating (PS)
5. Instructional assistives (e.g., computers, type-to-speak)
6. Tutoring: peer (P), volunteer (V), other elementary student (E)
7. One-on-one instruction with teacher (1-1)

Using this list, document the modification, noting the date and number as in the following example.

Modification Chart

Date	Curriculum Area	Modification	Comments
specific date, time	L.A.	**1-T** (denotes extra time on a test)	Add comments only if needed for this task.
specific date, time	M	4	Seems to work better if not seated by Jason.

Referrals

Every teacher, at some point in his or her career, must initiate a referral for exceptional education services. To learn this procedure, meet with the school guidance counselor or designated personnel early in the school year.

Before making a referral, review documentation on the student (see **Record Keeping**) to determine whether you have enough solid evidence for supporting the referral. Check your records for the modifications used and their results. Your evidence must show that you involved the parents and other stakeholders before requesting the referral. Be aware that referrals are a long and tedious process. Though not easy, proper documentation makes the process painless.

Reflection

Reviewing and assessing your teaching practice is crucial to growing professionally. By honestly reflecting on what went well during a lesson or classroom management situation and what didn't—and why it didn't—you can resolve problems and address ongoing concerns. For example, if your Open House did not go as planned, think about the questions parents asked following your presentation. What topics could be added to better inform parents and what elements might be omitted?

To help you reflect on lessons, make notes in your teacher's editions about the lessons. Using sticky notes or writing in the margins of the text, list what worked and what did not. Jot down ideas for future lessons on the subject and other insights for improving or augmenting the lesson. When it is time to plan the lesson again, you will see the reminder notes and remember! For related information regarding reflection, also see **Take Time to . . .**

Relationship Building

With students. Marzano and Marzano (2003) found that teachers who had strong relationships with their students had fewer discipline problems than teachers who did not. They suggested the following habits to build positive relationships with students:

- Greet students by name when they arrive to class.
- Compliment students (haircut, achievement, or sport accomplishment).

- Attend students' extracurricular activities. Students notice and are thrilled that you take the time to see them.
- Talk to students informally whenever possible.
- Ask questions about their interests.
- Listen, listen, listen!

Make students feel special

Students like to feel special. To show them that they are, I include activities in the classroom routine that promote personal attention, fun, or distinction to build relationships with my students. Those exclusive activities include:

- **Executive lunches.** Individual or group lunches forge a special bond between you and the students. Use a tablecloth or place mats to emphasize the special-ness of the occasion.
- **Student surveys.** My students enjoy developing surveys and polling their peers on likes and dislikes.
- **Individual reading or writing conferences.** One-on-one conferences are a great way to connect with each student.
- **Journal dialogues.** I read students' journal entries and personal narratives, and then write comments back to them.

—Sarah Wolfe Hartman, 3rd-Grade Teacher, Buckland
Mills Elementary School, Gainesville, Virginia

With parents. Building relationships with parents is well worth the extra effort, because partnering with parents is vital to helping a struggling student, acquiring that extra hand for a class project, or having enough parents for a special field trip. Developing rapport with parents is similar to the approaches used with students.

In this age of email and texts, personal notes have become even more special. Handwritten notes show you care. Encourage connection. You can ask parents to write you a letter about how their child is special. To persuade response, assign the letter as homework at Open House or Back-to-School Night, bribing parents with homework passes for their children if the letter is returned within a week's time.

Recipe for successful communication

2 cups of patience

2 cups of humility

2 ears for listening

1 heaping of nonjudgmental attitude

2 cups of love

2 cups of respect

2 cups of wisdom

Mix ingredients well with understanding and a willingness to do what's best for the child. Serve extra large portions. Even if this great recipe does not lead to perfect results, you can't go wrong starting out with ample portions of the best ingredients.

> *The only reason I always try to meet and know the parents better is because it helps me to forgive their children.*
>
> —Louis Johannot, former Director, Institut Le Rosey, Switzerland (1919–2009)

With the principal. Develop a good rapport with your principal, and you'll be at ease going to him or her with questions or difficult classroom situations. Communicate professionally. Invite the principal to your classroom for special events and keep him or her informed about your classroom concerns or difficult behaviors. For more information on working with a principal, see **Principles for Dealing with Principals**.

Rewarding Positive Behavior

How to reward appropriate behavior is a personal, philosophical question you must determine for yourself. As with many choices, there are pros and cons and differing opinions by experts. From retail rebates to good behavior parties in the classroom, reward systems are common in Western society. Despite this trend, some teachers and experts in the field believe that rewarding good behavior is merely bribing students to do what they should do anyway.

When considering the pros and cons of rewarding behavior, do keep in mind the value of intangible rewards. A positive phone call to parents, a word of encouragement, or an unexpected reward can be very effective. In fact, unexpected rewards work best. Varying what and when you reward keeps students on track because they never know when they might be rewarded. Also keep in mind that continual rewards lose their motivating power and may actually encourage Greed Monsters—students who won't make an effort unless a reward is involved.

If you decide to reward good behaviors, avoid focusing on immediate gratification or material returns. Plan out the type and frequency of rewards you will use. Start small and keep them simple, corresponding rewards and behaviors; do not reward commonly expected behaviors with grandiose rewards. When not overdone, stickers and prizes can be constructive, especially for young students.

If tangible rewards are not part of your management plan, determine other means for motivating students to follow the rules. Positive comments, gestures, and a smile when students display good behaviors provide simple, but powerful intangible rewards. Thank students for their efforts and give them a thumbs-up now and then, along with literal or figurative pats on the back. Praising students for jobs well done by pointing out a specific attribute of their work is most effective. Who wouldn't benefit from genuine and deserved feedback?

Role Model

As mentioned in **Reality Check,** your behavior influences students, and your role in students' lives places you in the unique position of modeling the type of person and citizen you would like each one to be someday. You do not have to be perfect by any means, but embrace the opportunity to model honesty, integrity, caring, and community to your still-growing and learning students.

> *Teachers with character serve as role models for telling the truth, respecting others, accepting and fulfilling responsibilities, playing fair, earning and returning trust, and living a moral life.*
> —Angela Lumpkin (2008), Professor, Health, Sport, and Exercise Sciences, University of Kansas

Routines

Routines are different from rules. A routine is the sum of various activities that you do somewhat automatically during a day because it has become a familiar pattern of behavior. Just as the activities that prepare you for your day have become routine, so should various classroom activities. Well-managed classrooms are that way because certain processes are so automatic that they make up the day's routine. Routines add stability and order to a student's life and are essential to a smooth–running classroom. Establishing routines takes time and patience, because they must be taught, practiced, and reinforced. Also see **Procedures Pave the Way**.

What's your routine?

- *Morning arrival*: backpacks and lunchboxes; attendance and lunch counts; daily announcements; homework submissions; daily agenda (see **Daily Agenda**)
- *Classroom time*: lining up; walking in the hall; bathroom; drinks of water; tissues; transitioning to and from lessons and groups; getting the teacher's attention; posting assignments; going to the clinic, office, specials, or exceptional education class; turning in papers; heading a paper; seeking assistance with a task; expectations when guests enter the classroom; emergencies; changing classes
- *Dismissal*: packing materials for homework; retrieving backpacks and lunchboxes; tidying desks and classroom areas before leaving

---

Rules

For a classroom that functions effectively, you must establish "expectations of appropriate student behavior" (Wong & Wong, 2005, p. 143). The Wongs strongly recommended numerous procedures anchored by three to five core classroom rules as the infrastructure of classroom management. A short list of rules is easy to remember and follow, so establish a few critical rules only for classroom behavior and let procedures help manage the rest (refer to **Procedures Pave the Way**).

Whether you form the rules alone or allow your students to help establish them, introducing rules during the first few days of the school year is essential. Set clear expectations and post the rules as a reminder. Listing behaviors you don't want from students is easy, but what a long list that might be! Besides, "Don't Lists" are negative and can give students an excuse for a poor behavior simply because it wasn't listed. Instead, take a proactive approach by listing positive expected behaviors. Reasonable and fair rules that support self-responsibility empower students and increase the likelihood of having followers.

For every rule, you must have a consequence that is delivered immediately when that rule is broken. Broken rules are inevitable, no matter how "good" your class is. Students are human, after all—even when they act like they're from another planet. How you handle infractions greatly influences the success of the rules. Effective consequences directly connect to rules in a manner that is logical and meaningful. Students must understand the connection for them to resume following the rules and managing their own behavior. Also see **Choices and Consequences.**

Rule box

Plus and minus rules

Don't call out. (Negative)

Raise your hand when you have something to share. (Positive)

Cause and effect

Broken rule: A student fails to raise her hand to speak.

Appropriate consequence: Teacher ignores what the student said and calls on someone else to respond.

Inappropriate consequence: Teacher sends the child to the principal.

Sarcasm

There is never a place for sarcasm in classroom management. Sarcastic comments are disrespectful to the student and do not accomplish anything positive. The use of sarcasm also leads students to believe that this is acceptable behavior for them to use.

Seating Arrangements

Think carefully about the seating arrangement in your classroom, yet realize that whatever arrangement you set up must change occasionally throughout the year. When deciding on an arrangement, keep the following suggestions in mind:

- Never place a victim next to a victimizer.
- Seat ESOL students in the middle of the room so they can observe the actions of other students.
- Place a new student next to a reliable student who can assist the new person.
- Seat visual- and hearing-impaired students near the front of the classroom (unless hearing loss is directional).
- Place disruptive students on your visually dominant side. For instance, when reading a book to the class, think about how you hold the book and the direction you look to see the pages. You need to be able to see these students while you read.
- Avoid noisy areas. Loud AC units and windows near playgrounds often distract students.

Seating Charts

Learn names rapidly with the aid of a seating chart. It's a must if you teach more than one group of students. Using small sticky notes for students' names on seating charts allows you to make quick and easy changes. You can keep the seating chart intact by covering it with a clear protector sheet.

Security

When children are at school, the school is responsible for their safety. To ensure a safe environment and preparedness for emergency situations, most schools have a policy and alert system for immediate lockdowns. Lockdown situations—where all students are brought into the classroom and the door is locked—include a stranger on campus or an abduction attempt by a noncustodial parent. Knowing the code and what you and the students must do during this alert is imperative. If your school does not have a specific policy in place, help get one implemented. Unexpected and emergency situations epitomize the extreme reasons for teachers to know where students are at all times.

Shopping

Local discount stores are favorite shopping places of teachers. For $5 or less, you can find a multitude of inexpensive items perfect for bulletin boards and crafts. Tap your creative side to make the most of items available. Could that $1 shower curtain be trimmed to cover a bookcase or work as the drape for a puppet theater? Yard sales also yield great bargains and creative options—from used books to alternative storage containers and materials for myriad projects. The possibilities are endless!

SLANT

You can help students self-manage their participation in classroom instruction by teaching them appropriate behaviors, as outlined by SLANT. Developed by the College of Education at the University of Kansas, SLANT is a mnemonic representing these behavior strategies:

Sit up (without slouching).

Lean forward and listen.

Activate thinking.

Name key information (answer teacher's questions, share ideas).

Track the teacher (follow the teacher rather than look around the room).

For effective use of SLANT, you must teach students the strategies and have them practice each prior to a lesson. When it comes time to SLANT, they will know what to do. For a poster of these strategies, go to www.behavioralinstitute.org/FreeDownloads/TIPS/SLANT_acronym.pdf.

Sleep

If some students are easily distracted, often off-task, or even fall asleep in class, they may not be getting enough ZZZs. The average elementary child requires approximately 10 hours of sleep per night, yet many children do not get this needed rest (Kovarik, 2007). Without adequate sleep, children get tired at school, have difficulty focusing on the lesson, are irritable and easily frustrated, and have trouble controlling their emotions and impulses (Dahl, 1996).

In fact, sleep deprivation and Attention Deficit Hyperactivity Disorder (ADHD) have similar symptoms. If a student is frequently falling asleep in class or continually distracted, you need to speak to the child and the child's parents. He or she may need to be tested, or it could be that adequate rest would alleviate many of the difficulties the student experiences.

Social Media

Help your students be responsible in their use of social media by teaching them "electronic etiquette" and safety guidelines (see also **Digital Citizenship**). Though you are not responsible and cannot control students' use of social media sites outside the classroom, you may be able to influence how they use these sites. If you hear of vicious texts or posts by or about your students, you certainly can discuss concerns with parents and administrators. If you use social media sites in classroom instruction, you can use the situation to not only explain school policy about usage, but also appropriate cyber behavior in and out of school. See **Bullying** and **Cyberbullying** for related material.

Sounds of Language

A student's first language or language spoken at home can influence his or her academic progress. Because home language can affect interpretation of English instruction and conversation, it is helpful to be aware of language differences and cultural influences among your students.

Know that not all cultures have the same sounds of language. For example, double Ls in a British English word such as "call" are sounded out; but in a Spanish word such as "calle" the two Ls are pronounced like a Y. As another example, Japanese students in English-speaking classrooms often have trouble with R, L, and V sounds. Also, "th" sounds in words such as "month" and "thought" are not native to the Japanese language. For a basic overview, also see esl.fis.edu/grammar/langdiff/index.htm.

Stealing

Don't be shocked if stealing occurs in your classroom. Though it is an unacceptable behavior, stealing is not uncommon among children. When incidents of stealing occur, use them as learning opportunities on the difference between right and wrong. Focus on the idea that your classroom is a community where trust is important and each person is respected.

If something is stolen in your classroom, tread carefully; proving theft is difficult. Sometimes students declare that an object has been stolen, only to discover later that they misplaced it. If a student is found with a missing object, he or she is likely to claim that the object was borrowed. Children often do not admit guilt out of fear for what will happen to them.

Rather than getting caught up in proving stealing and possibly escalating the situation, you might make a general request for the item to be returned as soon as possible. Allowing students to anonymously return allegedly stolen goods, they can save face, yet still correct their actions and do what is right. When stealing has occurred and the identity of the light-fingered borrower is known, be sure to address the issue privately.

> *No matter how disappointed you feel, try to deal with the problem without letting your emotions interfere. Also, keep public knowledge of the incident to a minimum.*
> —Thomas O. Jewett, retired Assistant Professor, McKendree College, Lebanon, Illinois

Student Jobs

Engage students, enhance their sense of belonging, streamline routines, and teach responsibility by setting up jobs in the classroom. Student jobs also can coordinate with your classroom economy. With "earnings" from their jobs, students can purchase items at the class store or auction. Post available positions and their pay rates, choosing age-appropriate responsibilities. Give older students a peek into adult life by having them fill out job applications that are rejected if they are messy, filled with spelling errors, or incomplete. Limit lengths of employment to allow students to try different duties.

Job openings

Sharpener of Pencils

Class Custodian

Board Cleaner

Horticulturist (plant keeper)

Messenger

Count/Countess of Lunches

Attendance Officer

Paper Distributor

Student Responses

Thought-provoking questions promote learning and critical thinking, so planning critical questions and how students can respond to them is a worthy investment of time. Responding with raised hands is only one appropriate solution. Rather than calling out answers or even responding when called on, students can write out their answers in a number of ways. Some teachers also use clickers to tally whole-group responses.

Whole-group responses

- *Clear sheet protectors.* Students can write on the slick outer surface with a non-permanent, dry-erase pen that can be wiped clean. To make whole–group responses easily visible to you, have students slide a blank piece of paper inside the folder.
- *White boards.* Use handmade white boards cut from a sheet of white shower board (the liner used prior to tiling). Cut enough boards for the students in your classroom. When purchasing the board, mention that you are a teacher, and the store personnel may cut it for you. Once cut, cover rough edges with colored masking tape. Note that even dry-erase markings must be cleaned off immediately after use. Students can erase responses with old socks, but rubbing alcohol and a multipurpose cleaner are needed for deeper cleanings. At the end of the school year, clean the boards with a rag soaked in lacquer thinner.

Students with Special Needs

Accommodating students with special needs applies to classroom management as well as academics. Work closely with your building's special education professionals and parents to develop the best behavior management plan for these students. The Individualized Education Program (IEP) should guide your efforts to help the child manage his or her behavior responsibly. You can expect children with behavior disorders to challenge you. Do not take this misbehavior personally; view their actions as inappropriate rather than seeing the students as difficult children. These children, whatever their challenges, deserve your respect and care. When these students act out, be patient with them and with yourself.

To learn about specific behavior management systems that have been successful for students with special needs, visit the website of the Council for Exceptional Children at www.cec.sped.org.

Substitute Teachers

If ever there is a time for classroom management challenges, it is when an unexpected teacher is in the room. Some students view this time as a chance to challenge the rules. Other students may act out because they feel insecure in the absence of their usual teacher. Though you may think you cannot possibly miss school your first year, it is in your students' best interest to plan now for a possible absence.

Preparing for a substitute. Have clear plans and directions for a substitute teacher to follow while you are out. Appoint student helpers to assist this teacher. Keep a copy of classroom rules, lesson plans, alternative activities, and helpful hints in a Guest Teacher packet, and store it in a prominent place so that it can be retrieved easily. Referring to a substitute teacher as a Guest Teacher helps students view this new teacher as someone else from whom they can learn rather than someone who is not their *real* teacher.

Being a substitute. Serving as a substitute teacher, that is, Guest Teacher, often is a stepping-stone to securing a position. Take advantage of such opportunities. Serving in this role helps you hone your professionalism. In the role of Guest Teacher, you learn to respond to new situations, meet other professionals, gain experience in different grade levels, and observe various types of classrooms. Be prepared for the role by having backup lessons and activities. Refer to *ABC's Online* for additional information regarding this topic.

Supplies

Even when school budgets are less restrictive than those in recent years, teachers often dip into their own pockets to purchase supplies for their classrooms. According to the National School Supply and Equipment Association's 2010 Retail Market

Awareness Study (NSSEA, 2010), teachers surveyed spent an average of $170 of their own money on school supplies and about $186 on instructional materials for a total of $356 in the 2009–2010 school year, compared to $395 in the 2007–2008 study and $552 in the 2005–2006 study.

Teachers indicated that they were spending less because of the economy. Whatever the economy is like when and where you teach, undoubtedly you too will dip into your pockets. Yet, it is not all up to you. You can ask parents to help with supplies, go to the school's parent-teacher organization for large items, and enlist help from the community when necessary.

In addition to listing items needed in your classroom newsletters, you might "plant" a giving tree in your room or plan a holiday gift exchange for which students bring a wrapped gift for the classroom. The giving tree is a tree branch bearing "leaves" that name a needed item. Students or parents may pluck a leaf of their choice. With a little creativity and bit of time, you can find the supplies you need to enhance classroom instruction. Volunteers may have some fun ideas and already have a network of people they can tap for classroom needs. P.S. Don't forget your thank-yous! Show gratitude as a class—have students write thank-you notes when items are received.

Take Time to . . .

. . . **care for yourself**. Seems obvious, doesn't it? Yet burnout happens! (See **Burnout**.) The first year especially can be overwhelming. When you step into the classroom, you become a facilitator of learning even while you still are learning so much yourself. Though on-the-job training is inherent in any first-time position, your training is multi-faceted. You also are establishing competency and comfort levels with students, colleagues, parents, administrators, and curriculum. For these reasons, self-care is recommended to ensure a balanced lifestyle (Gorrow & Muller, 2008).

Working in a service profession can be demanding, and many teachers tend to put their own needs last. Be sure to take time to care for yourself so that you retain the energy and dedication to continue helping others.

Self-care tips

1. *Seek mentors and resources.* Collaborate with your mentor to think through certain situations and brainstorm possible solutions to educational challenges. Investigate websites, education-related online bulletin boards, books, and articles for ideas, solutions, and connections.

2. *Nurture emotional health.* Focus on positive activities and solutions that help solve problems and emotionally recharge you. Sharing emotions can be a helpful release, but do so carefully. Maintain confidentiality. Talk privately without mentioning identifying information. Most of all, enjoy your life outside work.

3. *Sustain physical health.* Whether you walk, jog, garden, or dance, take time each week for physical activity to boost your immune system, mental sharpness, productivity, and overall well-being.

4. *Support mental health.* As simplistic as it seems, sometimes mind over matter is the best solution to challenges and frustrations. To prevent getting bogged down in situations, train yourself to look at difficulties as challenges—as professional puzzles in need of creative solutions. Look for positive qualities in each student and colleague, and be sure to document and celebrate successes.

—Andrea Sabatini McLoughlin, Associate Professor of
Education, Long Island University, Brookville, New York

... reflect on the effectiveness of your management strategies. Whether you write your observations in a journal to read at a later date, videotape yourself teaching a lesson, or discuss lessons and techniques with colleagues, reflection is vital to professional and personal growth (see also **Reflection**). Studying your classroom practices and student responses in an objective manner is critical to ongoing learning—both yours and that of your students—so incorporate reflection in your schedule early in the first year. Take time throughout the year to ask reflective questions, including the following ones, to help you assess your classroom as you learn your role.

- Are students improving their self-control?
- Do respect and community characterize your classroom?
- Are rules being followed?
- Is your classroom an effective learning environment?

If you answered "no" to any of these questions, dig deeper to discover what prevents you from achieving these goals. Write down what is right in your classroom and what is not as the first steps toward improving your practice. When you have feelings of failure, remember to keep mistakes in perspective—view them simply as new learning experiences.

If you feel stuck, seek assistance. You may need someone else to help you gain perspective and clarity. Your mentor or a trusted colleague could observe you in the classroom and give you feedback.

Getting perspective

- Set goals for instructional, professional, and personal growth.
- Connect with colleagues and find a mentor.
- Communicate with your principal.
- Get involved with the school and community.
- Keep a journal of your great lessons—and the not-so-great ones, too—for developing future lessons.
- Make time for sharing and planning.

> —Sarah Wolfe Hartman, 3rd-Grade Teacher, Buckland
> Mills Elementary School, Gainesville, Virginia

Tattling

It can try a sane person's patience! At the primary or elementary level, however, it comes with the territory. Young children tend to tattle, often believing that telling is actually the right thing to do—and it can be, when someone is hurt or involved in a dangerous situation. For every serious report, however, is a string of tattling from a certain few about who said what to whom that may or may not require teacher intervention. That's not to dismiss incident sharing; only to give it perspective and to address it.

Young students find it difficult to resist the urge to be first to let the teacher know who's done what. Because of that tendency, some teachers place a Book of Tattles in their rooms. Rather than running to the teacher with a tattle, students write out the tattle in a notebook that the teacher views later. Though eliminating tattling is unrealistic, you can tame the tattletale's torrent.

Taming the tattletale

- When a student begins to tattle, stop the conversation by asking, "Is anyone hurt?" If not, send the student back to work it out with that person.

- Assign a peer mediator. Encourage responsibility in students by having the tattletale talk about the situation with a student mediator. Because most incidents that trigger tattling occur during recess, lunch, or independent work time, a peer mediator is a great resource.
- Allow tattles to be shared during the regular class meeting. Students like the idea of being able to talk about the incident, but they usually forget about it by the next meeting.
- Give mini-lessons on getting along with others and resolving problems. Share stories representing these topics and provide activities that develop interpersonal skills.

Teacher Look

Don't overlook a silent but powerful classroom management tool: your facial expression. Most teachers develop the "teacher look"—the facial expression that effectively tells a student from across the room that his or her actions are not acceptable and to "stop." The teacher look is not taught; just know that you will develop yours quickly as you work within your classroom.

Teapot Syndrome

"Shh." Then the teacher adds a little longer "shhh." When that doesn't work, another four or five more are added. "Shh. Shh. Shh, shh." It's called the teapot syndrome—because the teacher sounds like a teapot! What's more, "shh" is not an effective quieting technique. Said too many times, it simply becomes white noise, background that students do not notice. The **Teacher Look** and other strategies are more effective (see **Whole Class Attention**).

Teasing and Taunting

Though there is no harm in allowing children to joke around with one another, there comes a point when teasing switches from light-hearted joking to cruel insults. It is important for you to step in when the behavior moves to an unacceptable level and let students know that the behavior must stop immediately. If it continues after your intervention, you need to implement consequences appropriate to the situation and age of the student.

If you joke in a teasing way with students, be careful what you say and how you say it. Your words cannot be hurtful or misconstrued. As the role model for your students, you do not want to model inappropriate behaviors. Most students desperately want to be liked and accepted by their teachers. Gentle teasing may be acceptable; however, humor comes in many forms, so encourage positive humor that uplifts and includes rather than run the risk of hurting feelings.

Telephone

Share your school phone number with parents, along with the times you are available. You may want to keep your home and cell phone numbers private. After all, teachers need a break also! For related information, see **Parents** and **Cell Phones**.

Testing

Students often become anxious about tests, especially standardized tests that extend over several days. Some test anxiety comes from not knowing what to expect. To ease students' fear of the unknown, familiarize them with the format of the test ahead of time using samples from the testing companies, so they can concentrate on content during the actual testing. Help students cope with the pressure of being timed by giving practice timed tests and encouraging a sense of rising to a challenge rather than fearing the "ticking clock."

When testing time comes, encourage your students to eat a good breakfast. Parents might be willing to send in wholesome snacks as a special treat. Prepare yourself by becoming familiar enough with the test's format and directions to remain calm and in control as you administer the test. Answering students' questions clearly and confidently reassures them. Incorporate into the days of testing tension-releasing activities, such as stretches, deep breathing exercises, calisthenics, and outdoor games to give students an outlet and help them focus on the test.

At the end of the day's testing, acknowledge their efforts with a special activity, such as extra recess time, a class kickball game, relay races, or a walk outside the building.

Testing dividers

Straying eyes during quizzes and tests can occur easily among elementary students. To help students do their own work, construct a test divider to create a private desk area. Take three file folders, opening up two and laying them flat with a space between them. Next, lay the third file folder on top so that the two sides lie on top of the right and left sides of the other folders. Then glue or tape the middle sections, one on top of the other. Voilà, the private testing area is finished! It also folds and stacks easily for storage.

Textbooks

Help students get the most they can from their textbooks; teach them about textbook format. Explain that bold words represent key items to know and that they usually are on chapter tests. Point out that the first sentence in each subheading generally highlights what the paragraph is about. This knowledge is not intuitive; help students learn to learn by pointing out contextual clues. As you teach, keep in mind that younger students must be taught how to use picture clues and older students must be taught how to take notes. Developing these skills is imperative because they are crucial to students' ongoing academic success.

Time-on-Task Study

If you have a student in your class who is having behavioral or academic issues, consider completing a time–on–task study. Tracking a student's behavior provides insights into patterns of behaviors. The data from the study then informs the next steps to be taken to assist the student.

Time Tracker

Time-on-Task Study

Student's Name _____

Date _____

Time	On-Task	Off-Task	Commitments/Time Off

Before conducting the study, note whether the study difficulties tend to occur during a particular time of the day, such as after lunch, to help you determine a time frame for the study. For best results, ask the guidance counselor or a colleague to observe the student for one lesson during that time frame. Have the observer record the student's times on and off task for set time increments (e.g., every 2 minutes for a 30-minute lesson). For the times off task, the observer also should note what occurred that may have triggered the loss of focus: *John asked Tim a question.* Calculate the percentage of time on- and off-task from the data gathered for factual reference when speaking with parents or referring the student to a study team.

Time-Out

If any management strategy is overused and abused, it is time-out. Doled out too frequently, time-out loses its value and purpose of improving behavior. For time-out to be effective, time-in must be more appealing. You, the teacher, set the length of time, not the student. Be sure the time-out spot you designate is highly visible, yet separated enough from activities to help the student refocus and be able to return to the tasks at hand. A student's return to time-in must be a "nonevent"—a quick welcome without scolding or negativity.

A student already making poor choices does not suddenly make good ones, so you may have to turn to other management techniques if time-out is no longer effective for a particular student.

Time-Savers

Attendance. Check attendance quickly with "name sticks." Near the entrance to the classroom, place a container of Popsicle sticks, each one bearing the name of a student. A second similar container is placed on your desk. When students arrive to class, they move their stick from the container by the door to the can on your desk. Seeing who is absent is as simple as checking the container by the classroom door.

Grading. When appropriate, have students grade their own papers during class time. Set up a few pass/zero assignments in which successfully completed assignments receive a passing grade and incomplete assignments get a zero. Give partial points to partially completed assignments. For less tedious grading, divide writing assignments and long projects into several small steps.

In upper elementary, assign students a number that corresponds to their name alphabetically and have them place that number in the top right corner of their papers. When assignments are collected, a student helper can arrange the papers in numerical order so that when you grade the papers, you can easily enter scores in your grade book. Also see **Grading**.

Organization. Hunting and gathering seem to be the biggest time wasters for many teachers. With a wide variety of lessons to teach and tasks to accomplish, you want your focus on teaching and learning. From lesson materials and supplies to "do lists" and errand running, organization is the underlying ingredient to time-saving. Also see the related alpha entries **Juggling Paperwork**, **Organization**, and **Helping Tools**.

Paperwork. Daily classroom life is overflowing with papers. Assignment notebooks, binders, student mailboxes, and plastic crates are all proven tools for helping students get organized. They also may help you to track and organize the flood of papers.

Paperwork pointer

Monthly paper files, subdivided into days (1–31), keep me organized. When a form, notice, email, or letter comes in that must be addressed, I file it in the appropriate date. Then I add a reminder to my planner that includes details. For example, if I get word that an assembly is scheduled for May 17 in the gym, and my class is to leave at 9:04 and sit in row 5, I jot "9:04 to gym" in my planner or PDA and place the notice describing the event in the file. Each day, I pull the next day's file folder to keep on my desk as reference.

> —Theresa Knipstein Meyer, Instructor and Director of the
> Alternative Accelerated Program in Special Education at
> Butler University, Indianapolis, Indiana

Supplies. Designate a shelf or container for extra classroom supplies, such as tape, staples, scissors, and glue. When students need one of those items, they can retrieve it from the Supply Spot rather than rummaging through the classroom closet or your desk!

Technology. Save time, save a tree—go electronic. As much as possible, keep electronic records and communications with colleagues and parents. Embrace technology and record grades on your computer. Send notes to parents via email or the class website, but do provide an alternative for students and parents who do not have computers. Make use of a homework hotline. Spend a little bit of time searching recommended websites for ideas, experiments, and lesson plans to incorporate into your curriculum, and develop lesson plans on the computer. Have tech-savvy students assist you with your classroom site's posts. Don't be intimidated; learn from them.

Transitions

Moving from one curriculum topic to another one does not just happen; teachers must plan transitions. Without planned strategies, transitions can be a classroom management fiasco. It was for one young educator observed by her administrator. Though her well-planned lesson went very well, introducing the next lesson did not, and she struggled to get students refocused on the next lesson—students just did not make the transition.

Transitions must be managed, just as lessons are. Transition from lesson to lesson, independent work to whole-class discussion, and lessons to lunch (or vice versa) in numerous ways, fitting the transition to the activity when suitable. You can use **Quick-and-Easy Attention Grabbers** to assist transitions, especially when students are moving from their desks to another area. One effective lesson transition is Countdown.

Countdown

Teacher: "It is time to put away your science books and move to math. You will have 10 seconds to get out your math book and turn to page 73 (number also is written on the board). You need a pencil too. You must be ready when I reach zero. I am starting the count now. "Ten . . . nine . . . eight . . . ."

Situations that require students to line up, such as lunch, recess, or physical education class, allow a chance to have fun with the transition. You might call out colors of clothing, birthday months, or even questions for which correct responders get in line. If lining up does not go well, have students sit down and try again. With many students traveling in the hallway, orderliness is important. Good teachers plan for and teach transitions.

Undesirable Behaviors

When students continually exhibit unacceptable behaviors, there is an underlying reason. Whether an irritating habit, aggressive behavior, or lying, the behavior serves the student in some way. As mentioned previously, that behavior is driven by a need for attention, power, revenge, or inadequacy (Dreikurs et al., 2004).

Recognizing the motivating need behind the misbehavior helps you gauge a proper response without fulfilling the sought-after need. Look for clues to help the student learn healthy alternatives in getting his or her needs met.

Students who misbehave simply to get *any* type of attention should receive attention only when they don't act out. Watch for positive behavior from these students and make a point to compliment them. Offer a word of praise for positive behavior even if it is unrelated to the misbehavior. Compliment the student when he or she uses proper manners, shares a snack, or uncharacteristically raises his or her hand before speaking.

Unresponsive Parents

It is frustrating when you need parents' help in meeting their child's needs and they are unresponsive. However, you must be extra diligent in keeping uninvolved parents informed on their child's progress and behavior. Though you may question why you should try so much when the parents don't, continue your efforts anyway. What you do is for the student. Call, send notes or emails, and set up mini-conferences to discuss your concerns. You never know when your perseverance will pay off. More important, you may be the only one standing in that child's corner.

Using Resources

More than ever before, excellent teaching takes teamwork. At times you may feel as though you are flying solo in your teaching, but know that you have a support system behind you. Draw on and use the various resources available to you—in your school and community and through professional organizations and their online communities. Look to a peer teacher you respect, an assigned mentor, guidance counselor, child study team, and the administrative team for assistance. Gain knowledge and help from excellent educational content and community sites, such as www.kdp.org. Remember, it is alright to ask for help. Taking a proactive approach to challenges and unresolved problems advances your professional knowledge and capabilities to create a continually improving classroom environment.

Victim and Victimizer

Upper elementary students can be mean to one another. Be careful not to place a victim and victimizer close to each other when assigning groups or arranging seating. Get in the habit of pointing out commonalities among students who fall into these roles to encourage a common bond and understanding.

Violence

A violent incident is every teacher's most serious concern. When faced with the threat of violence, your first responsibility is to ensure the safety of the students in your care. Don't try to be a hero or martyr, but do everything possible to keep students safe.

School policy. Know your school's policy for dealing with violent behavior so that you won't be caught off guard. Aside from the process outlined by your school, there is not one particular step-by-step formula for dealing with violence that you have to follow. There are general precautions to prevent escalation of violence, but each situation is different. Remaining calm, using common sense, and having patience should be your first line of defense.

If a student—or anyone—becomes violent, concentrate on being composed. The last thing you want to do is to agitate the offender; that only escalates the situation. Calmly, but firmly, try to talk the offender into settling down and refraining from a violent act. If a weapon is involved, keep your distance and do not make quick moves.

Calming demeanor. If possible, get the other students out of the classroom or at least away from the offender. Work out an emergency plan that includes a signal between you and a few students that cues someone to go for help. A specific phrase, code, or motion is important in potentially unstable situations. The volatility of the situation should determine the practicality of such an action, but an initial plan is valuable. Remaining collected is the best approach when attempting to get the offender to calm down or release a weapon. As you wait for help, keeping the offender talking can deter further violent actions.

No matter which strategies your school district uses for reducing the threat of violence, you can employ techniques within your classroom to shape a nonthreatening community. Establish a positive and caring learning environment where differences are respected, guiding students to realize what that means to them personally. Help them learn to trust and to give respect. Also, let students know that they can come to you when they need help. If you suspect that a student may be involved in a gang or violent behavior, share your concerns with the proper authorities as required by school and civil policies. Report any student who seems increasingly angry or who loses control frequently or with mounting aggression. Intervention may be necessary.

When a student acts violently

1. Immediately command the student to stop.
2. Using his or her name, command the student to sit down.
3. Ensure the safety of other students. If possible, send them out of the room. Also consider your own safety by putting distance between you and the offending student, but continue telling the student precisely what to do.
4. Get help from an administrator, school security, or the police in controlling the student.
5. Follow pre-established consequences and corrective actions as well as school policies regarding violent behavior.
6. Document the incident in detail and duplicate copies of the report.
7. Arrange for the student to get special help with anger management.

—Pamela Kramer Ertel, Co-author, *The ABC's of Classroom Management*

Violence Prevention

The goal of any level of classroom management is prevention, and preventing violence is part of the plan. Ryan (2008) recommended a strong violence prevention program for all school districts, which follows these strategies:

- Focus on strong academic goals.
- Model appropriate behavior.

- Discourage and intervene in behaviors that lead to violence.
- Do not tolerate inappropriate behavior.
- Provide direct counseling.
- Train staff to address behavior problems in the classrooms.
- Avoid knee-jerk reactions to behavioral challenges.
- Address behavioral issues in private and do not humiliate students in public.
- Find ways to help *all* students feel appreciated and valued.
- Create a classroom environment of mutual respect.
- Generate a climate of inclusiveness in classrooms and the school.
- Hold students accountable for their behavior.

Programs for preventing violence and bullying should be school-wide, but a supportive and caring community begins in each classroom. The rules and expectations you put into practice to manage the environment work alongside these prevention strategies and are augmented by the extras you do to make students feel special and part of your classroom community. Creating and tending a caring environment gives students a sense of safety, something some students may not experience at home. You want your students to feel comfortable coming to you about their problems. When they do, act on what you can address and seek other professional support personnel to deal with situations beyond the scope of your role as classroom educator.

Voice

You have a voice—in your classroom and the learning environment—no matter how soft-spoken you may believe you are. In fact, your voice is your most powerful tool! It can quiet a loud classroom with barely a whisper; when you speak softly, students must quiet down to hear you. Your voice in song can gain attention. Even if you can't sing, try it anyway. It still will get students' attention and may provide a moment of comic relief to the day!

Your voice speaks for others. Because you are a teacher, you also have a voice for your students, your professional work, and educational practices. You can advocate for all of them and at various levels—with parents, to administrators, around the community, and even in the legislature. Though exercising your voice may not be directly related to managing your classroom, it is an extension of your role in the profession. Your voice is an instrument, and you can use it effectively.

> ❝ *As the ones accountable for implementing policy decisions, teachers have a responsibility to stay current on topics of reform at both the local and national levels.*
>
> —Anna Shults, 2007 Indiana Teacher of the Year and Literacy Specialist, Indiana Department of Education ❞

Volunteers

So often teachers could use help in the classroom, yet they tend to view having volunteers as more work. Don't miss out on extra hands in your classroom—plan ahead. Preparation is the secret to having willing volunteers and productive results. When you take time to set up specific projects or ongoing activities and provide accompanying instruction sheets for them, volunteers can jump into working and you won't have to be pulled from teaching.

Consider setting up volunteer training sessions for activities that need more explanation or that require specific techniques. Training volunteers in educationally sound techniques to enhance reading or math skills is a long-term investment in both student and volunteer success. Volunteers who are well prepared and believe they are making a difference through their efforts continue to volunteer.

First things first! Before your first volunteer enters the classroom, be sure you have obtained approval. Be informed on your school's policy. Most districts require fingerprints, background checks, and a signed form on file. Some schools do not allow volunteers to work alone with students; they must be supervised by a certified teacher. The ultimate consideration is the safety and well-being of students.

Volunteer box

Design a volunteer box, a "treasure chest" of tasks and projects, accompanied by a set of directions. Let parents know about the volunteer box through a class newsletter or special note, inviting them to visit the classroom and choose one of its "treasures." If you place the box near the entrance to the classroom, volunteers can grab a project without interrupting the flow of instructional time. Be sure to include both in-school and take-home projects and tasks to accommodate the schedules of your parent, grandparent, and community volunteers.

Water

Add water to your recipe for good classroom management. Keeping hydrated is essential to successful instruction and learning, because human brains are approximately 70% water, and they need water to function well. Dehydrated bodies can lead to impaired thought processes. Water is especially important in the morning, as is a good breakfast. It fuels the body and mind for the day. You inevitably will have students who arrive at school without an adequate breakfast or fluid intake; therefore, it is doubly important for them to rehydrate. Water is essential after recess too.

When possible, allow students to access water throughout the day. You might have them bring a water bottle labeled with their name to keep at their desk. Set guidelines about when it can be refilled, designating a routine for it as you do for pencil sharpening. If your school does not allow water bottles, develop a procedure for water fountain breaks.

Also keep in mind that some students may have special requirements regarding water. Children with diabetes must have water frequently throughout the day. During Ramadan, Muslim students are not allowed to drink any beverage, including water, from sunrise to sunset. Special situations like this requires teachers to plan accordingly for recess periods, especially during hot weather.

Websites for Your Classroom

Many Internet sites offer teachers free hosting for a classroom website. If you establish a classroom website, be sure to keep it updated and reflective of events occurring in your classroom. Follow your school's guidelines and, when possible, have students contribute and assist with updates.

Websites with Wisdom

> 66 *No man is wise enough by himself.*
> —Titus Maccius Plautus, ancient Roman
> Playwright (c. 254–184 BC) 99

When you need a word from the wise and your mentor is unavailable, keep in mind that good advice, tips, and knowledge are merely a URL away. Search recommended websites for what you need, whether it's ideas for lesson plans, techniques for coping with specific behaviors, or strategies from veteran teachers. You can find recommendations in the **Resources** section of this book, at *ABC's Online,* and always in the Resources site at KDP Online, www.kdp.org/teachingresources.

Weekly Folder

Many schools require teachers to send home weekly folders as part of their school–home communication strategy—to keep parents regularly informed on their students' work and progress. To prepare these folders, students place their work in their folders throughout the week and then take them home on Friday. At home, parents are to review the contents and sign a paper attached to the folder to indicate they have seen the materials. Students return the folder to school the following Monday. If parents claim they have never seen the student's folder, you may need to get the administration's permission to mail them through the postal service.

Wellness

Organizing and maintaining your classroom includes being aware of and prepared for the medical needs of your students and possible medical emergencies. Give your room and yourself a wellness check-up.

Check-up

- **Review student medical-information cards.** Be aware of students' health concerns: allergies to food, insect bites, bee stings, and airborne contaminants. Know which students have medical conditions, such as ADHD, asthma, diabetes, epilepsy, and heart conditions.

- **Create a class medical list.** Ask the school nurse or office personnel for medical information about your students. Using that information, make a list, including the student's name, the nature of the concern, and its required treatment and medication. Be sure to have the medicine's exact name, dosage, and frequency.

- **Share list appropriately.** Place copies of the list in your plan book and substitute teacher folder, and share the list with your students' other teachers. Let the cafeteria manager know about students' food allergies. Be discriminating when sharing the list, because medical information is confidential and you must safeguard students' privacy.

- **Check the school policy on medication.** Learn the school's procedure for administering medicine at school and on field trips. Most schools have specific forms for logging the time the medication was administered, the dosage, and the method (e.g., oral), which usually must be submitted to the clinic at the end of the field trip.

- **Learn care procedures.** Knowing basic first aid is important, but you also must know the steps to take should a student with medical concerns have a severe reaction—as with children who have diabetes, severe allergies, or are prone to seizures. For example, you need to know how to administer an EpiPen in case a student with severe allergic reactions to stings has a run-in with a bee. First aid and CPR classes are recommended and may be required.

- **Plan ahead for emergencies.** Learn the school's procedure for a medical emergency, including moving from the classroom or playground to the clinic, and then plan your classroom emergency plan from it. When going to recess, for example, you may decide that it's helpful to carry a clipboard with your class list of medical information, clinic passes, and a pen.

—Madeline Kovarik, Co-author, *The ABC's of Classroom Management*

Whole Class Attention

Quickly gaining the attention of all students at once is significant in managing the classroom. Consider this scenario: The class is working, with some students at their desks, a few at centers, and others participating in a small group with you. You have been concentrating so much on the small group that you lost track of time and now realize it's time for school pictures! A quick departure is essential. How do you get their attention so that students gather and depart expediently? These strategies have worked well for many elementary teachers:

- **Give me five.** Say "give me five" and hold up your hand with fingers open. As soon as the students hear the command, they also raise their hand. The teacher then counts down (5, 4, etc.), lowering a finger on each count.
- **Call and recall.** Say a predetermined phrase that calls for a student response. For example, You say, "We are …," and the students respond "number one." This call-out is repeated three times.
- **Clap.** Clap a pattern that the students know to repeat or designate the pattern in the moment. For example, "Clap once if you can hear me (clap); clap twice if you can hear me (clap, clap); and clap three times if you can hear me (clap, clap, clap)."
- **Hand-raise.** Moving to the front of the classroom, raise your hand, and place a finger of your other hand to your lips to perform a silent "shh." If you taught students this procedure, they know to quit talking, stop what they are doing, and raise a hand too.
- **Chimes.** Sound a chime for an effective and peaceful way to gain the entire class's attention.
- **Simon Says.** Simply pick an action, such as touching your head, and say "If you can hear me, do this." Students must look at you to know what to do. Repeat three times with three different actions.

Withitness

Guillaume (2004) suggested that misbehavior happens more frequently when students believe the teacher cannot see them. With that concept in mind, be sure to demonstrate that you know what's going on with students. Be an alert teacher; show your "withitness" (Kounin, 1977). Frequently circulating the room keeps you with it, and your mere presence deters students from misbehaving. When you notice misbehavior, your official "silent look" tells a student to change the behavior. Once students know you are on to them, they are less likely to test you.

Work by Students

Ungraded student work easily can pile up to the size of small mountains. Before paperwork gets to that point, tackle it. Start with papers that can be graded the quickest—assignments with clear, specific answers, such as math papers. Grade that work, and record it in the grade book. Next, grade those papers requiring more time, such as essays or reports. To ease the grading process for those assignments, set up and follow a clear rubric for required elements. For example, if the response to an essay question must include three major points, place a check mark in the outer column each time you read a point. By the end of the paper, you will be able to easily identify whether the student reached the desired goal.

X-amine Your Bias

If you are human, you have a bias, whether it's a favorite color, style of clothing, or assumptions about people. Biases carry over into teaching without you even recognizing it. Some teachers might call on boys more than girls, or the right side of the classroom more than the left, and not know it. To become aware of unintentional bias, educational coaches recommend that teachers regularly videotape themselves. Intended for your eyes only, this recording serves as a private observation and professional development session. Watch it critically, noting any actions that may show bias. Becoming aware of and then working to overcome bias leads to a more equitable classroom environment.

X-pect to Be Tested

Your students will test you, especially in the area of classroom management. They will see how far they can push you, whether you are consistent, and whether you mean what you say. Why? Because you are a teacher, you are new to them, and they're kids! Don't feel like you have to be a drill sergeant to command respect, but do be firm. Above all, be consistent. Don't suggest a consequence you can't carry out. Making idle threats has gotten many beginning teachers in a bind. Once students realize threats won't be followed through, they have victory! When setting consequences, choose options you can and will implement.

X-tra Efforts Pay Off

Though your students may not admit it, they typically appreciate the extra efforts you make to help and connect with them. They welcome your efforts that show you care. When you see that someone is troubled, it may mean the world to that student for you to say, "Is there anything I can do to help?"

Take a few minutes daily to converse casually with your students. Ask the soccer player how the season is going; listen to the girl anxious to tell you about the movie she saw over the weekend. Sprinkle compliments around the room. Praise is powerful!

Extend extra effort to parents. Help them feel welcome in and important to your classroom. Pass along a positive comment about their child. Calling or emailing parents good news cultivates an affirming relationship with parents and students. Build a good relationship that sustains a conversation about less positive behavior. When students believe you truly care about them, they are more likely to be respectful.

Y Is a Good Question

"Why do we have to do this?" or "Why do we have to learn about that?" are common *why* questions students ask. *Why* questions sometimes seem disrespectful, but they need not be. When students understand the purpose of a rule, lesson, or assignment, they relate better to what is being asked of them and are more likely to engage in the activities. If you explain the rationale behind the rule or activity when introducing it, you can avoid *why* questions later.

Yelling

Yelling does not work! It is impossible for your voice to speak over the buzz in a classroom of 20 students. Do not fall into the trap of talking louder and louder to get everyone's attention. Use **Attention** devices instead. Also see **Whole Class Attention**.

You Can Do It!

If you are feeling fearful, beware. Students are keenly intuitive. Do everything in your power to mask your fears and appear confident. Don't let them see you sweat, or they will seize the opportunity to walk all over you. Remind yourself that you are the adult and that you are in control, even if you don't feel that way. You do have the final say about what happens in your classroom.

"You" Statements

With the varied challenges teachers encounter throughout the year, they can, at times, get down about their choice of profession. It might be comments from an unfriendly parent or a critical colleague or a sense of not being able to resolve students' problems. Being able to bounce back is critical to their well-being and sustainability in the profession. That's where *you* statements help. To lift your spirits and remind yourself of what you have done well, develop a personal folder of notes, drawings, affirming phrases, and pictures that connote, "Hey, you're doing a good job."

Add "you're my favorite teacher" cards or pictures and some inspirational quotes too. There's nothing like the notes and artwork of your students to remind you of the important contributions you make in students' lives. When you need a boost, go through the file and reread your *you* statements. Additionally, keep in mind that not everyone will see situations as you do—and you don't have to see things their way. Take advice when needed, but recognize that you are an expert and professional; you earned your teaching degree.

Zest

Now that you have many classroom management tools to use, you can put them into practice. Enter your classroom armed with this book, confidence, and a zest for teaching! You'll be great!

Zingers

Many teachers show their sense of humor through quips they make to students. Unfortunately, these remarks often slip into zingers—sarcastic or critical comments meant to be witty, but inappropriate when directed at students. Wit and humor that draw smiles or laughter refresh you and the students. Zingers detract from your professionalism, perhaps putting you at the students' level, and risk offending someone. Stick to professionalism and wit.

Zingers

Are you cruisin' for a bruisin'?

Shut your mouth.

Don't make me come over there!

I'm sick of your face.

Shut up!

Profanity

> *Most of the trouble and friction among people, in or out of school, is caused by putting others down.*
> —William Glasser, American Psychiatrist, developer of reality therapy and choice theory

Zone

You can expect your first year to be full of ups and downs, excitement and challenges, and trials interspersed with inevitable errors. Use the resources at hand. Seek help when needed. Reflect on your practice to celebrate successes and address areas where improvement is required. As you build skills and confidence, you will find your teaching zone—those optimal moments where teaching and learning just "click," where you and your students soar to new heights. Catch the zone!

Z—Last Letter in the Alphabet, Last Word in Classroom Management

Now that you have covered classroom management from A–Z, you can enter your classroom as an expert with all the answers. Right? If only it were that simple! Sorry, but that is not the message of this book—or reality in the classroom.

From A–Z, this book has shown you various techniques for running a classroom that you can apply immediately or transform into a style that works best for you. It also has directed you to other resources for strategies and ideas not included here.

In the end, this book is a tool and a guide, not a magic wand. Becoming an effective classroom manager is a process, a journey. With each group of students, you'll encounter something new. When a lesson doesn't go well or a student gets the best of you, learn from what happened and let it go. Start over the next day and leave the past behind.

References

Albert, L. (1989). *A teacher's guide to cooperative discipline: How to manage your classroom and promote self-esteem.* Circle Pines, MN: American Guidance Service.

Albert, L. (1996). *Cooperative discipline.* Lake Pines, MN: American Guidance Service.

Bartzis, O. L., & Hayner, A. (2009, April). *"Cheating" or "sharing"? Academic ethics across cultures.* Presentation at AACRAO conference, Chicago.

Batsche, G. M., & Knoff, H. M. (1994). Bullies and their victims: Understanding a pervasive problem in the schools. *School Psychology Review, 23*(2), 165–75.

Bloom, B. S., Engelhart, M. D., Furst, E. J., Hill, W. H., & Krathwohl, D. R. (1956). *Taxonomy of educational objectives: The classification of educational goals.* New York: Longmans, Green.

Broadbear, B. C., & Broadbear, J. T. (2000). Development of conflict resolution skills in infancy and early childhood. *The International Electronic Journal of Health Education, 3*(4), 284–90.

Charles, C. M. (2005). *Building classroom discipline* (8th ed.). Boston, MA: Allyn & Bacon.

Craig, D. I. (2003). Brain-compatible learning: Principles and applications in athletic training. *Journal of Athletic Training, 38*(4), 342–349.

Dahl, R. E. (1996). The impact of inadequate sleep on children's daytime cognitive function. *Seminars in Pediatric Neurology, 3*(1), 44–50.

DeVries, D., & Slavin, R. (1978). Teams-games-tournaments (TGT): Review of ten classroom experiments. *Journal of Research and Development in Education, 12,* 28–38.

Dreikurs, R. (1968). *Psychology in the classroom* (2nd ed.). New York: Harper & Row.

Dreikurs, R., Cassel, P., & Ferguson, E. D. (2004). *Discipline without tears: How to reduce conflict and establish cooperation in the classroom* (Rev. ed.). Hoboken, NJ: Wiley.

Dukes, R. L., & Albanesi, H. (2012). Seeing red: Quality of an essay, color of the grading pen, and student reactions to the grading process. *The Social Science Journal, 49.* Retrieved from http://dx.doi.org/10.1016/j.soscij.2012.07.005

Erwin, J. C. (2003). Giving students what they need. *Educational Leadership, 61*(1), 19–23.

Ginott, H. G. (1972). *Teacher and child: A book for parents and teachers.* New York: Macmillan.

Gordon, T. (2003). *Teacher effectiveness training.* New York: Three Rivers Press.

Gordon, J. (2007). *The energy bus.* Hoboken, NJ: Wiley.

Gordon, J. (2008). *The no complaining rule: Positive ways to deal with negativity at work.* Hoboken, NJ: Wiley.

Gorrow, T. R., & Muller, S. M. (2008). *The ABC's of wellness for teachers: An A–Z guide to improving your well-being in the classroom and out.* Indianapolis, IN: Kappa Delta Pi, International Honor Society in Education.

Guillaume, A. M. (2004). *K–12 classroom teaching: A primer for new professionals* (2nd ed.). Upper Saddle River, NJ: Pearson.

Jackson, M. F., & Joyce, D. M. (2003). *The role of music in classroom management*. New York: New York University.

Kounin, J. S. (1977). *Discipline and group management in classrooms*. Huntington, NY: R. E. Krieger.

Kovarik, M. (2007). House calls: Why sleep matters to your child. *National Health Review*, *(2)*1, 1–4.

Kriete, R. (2003). Start the day with community. *Educational Leadership, 61*(1), 68–70.

Leonard, M. (2012). Know your kids: Signs your kid may be in a gang [video]. Retrieved from www.gangsrreal.com

Lumpkin, A. (2008). Teachers as role models teaching character and moral virtues. *Journal of Physical Education, Recreation and Dance, 79*(2), 45–49.

Lyman, F. T. (1981). The responsive classroom discussion: The inclusion of all students. In A. Anderson (Ed.), *Mainstreaming Digest* (pp. 109–113). College Park: University of Maryland Press.

Marzano, R. J., & Marzano, J. S. (2003). The key to classroom management. *Educational Leadership, 61*(1), 6–13.

McIntyre, T. (2004). Strategies for teaching youth with ADD and ADHD. Retrieved from www.behavioradvisor.com/AddStrats.html

Moyer, K. E., & von Haller Gilmer, B. (1954). The concept of attention spans in children. *The Elementary School Journal, 54*(8), 464–66. Chicago: The University of Chicago Press.

National School Supply and Equipment Association. (2010). *The complete K–12 report: Market facts and segment analyses*. Rockaway Park, NY: Education Market Research.

Online Safety and Technology Working Group. (2010). Youth safety on a living Internet. Washington, DC: OSTWG. Retrieved from http://www.ntia.doc.gov/report/2010/youth-safety-living-internet

Owasso Independent School District No. I011 v. Falvo, 534 U.S.C. 426 (2002).

Preskill, S. L., & Jacobvitz, R. S. (2001). *Stories of teaching: A foundation for educational renewal*. Upper Saddle River, NJ: Pearson.

Rao, Y. (2010, September 5). Teaching is not a job, but a calling: Grace Pinto. *DNA: Daily News and Analysis*. Retrieved from www.dnaindia.com/academy/interview_teaching-is-not-a-job-but-a-calling-grace-pinto_1433633

Ribble, M. (2012). Digital citizenship for educational change. *Kappa Delta Pi Record, 48*(4), 148–51. doi: 10.1080/00228958.2012.734015.

Roebuck, E. (2002). Beat the drum lightly: Reflections on Ginott. *Music Educators Journal, 88*(5), 40–44.

Routier, W. J. (2003, May). *Read me a song: Teaching reading using picture book songs*. Paper presented at the Annual Meeting of the International Reading Association, Orlando, FL. Retrieved from www.eric.ed.gov/ERICWebPortal/contentdelivery/servlet/ERICServlet?accno=ED479645

Ryan, M. (2008). *Ask the teacher: A practitioner's guide to teaching and learning in the diverse classroom*. Boston: Pearson/Allyn and Bacon.

Strom, P., & Strom, R. (2005). Cyberbullying by adolescents: A preliminary assessment. *The Educational Forum, 70*(1), 21–36.

U.S. Department of Health and Human Services. (2012). *What is bullying.* Retrieved from www.stopbullying.gov/what-is-bullying

Wong, H. K., & Wong, R. T. (2005). *The first days of school: How to be an effective teacher* (CD-ROM ed.). Mountain View, CA: Harry K. Wong Publications.

Extras

Resources

ABC's Online

www.kdp.org/teachingresources/ABConline.php

The companion site to *The ABC's of Classroom Management* offers more detailed information on subjects, as designated in the alpha entry, links to related topics, and downloadable resources for novice educators.

Advocacy

www.kdp.org/aboutkdp/publicpolicy.php

The Public Policy and Advocacy website for Kappa Delta Pi, International Honor Society in Education, offers webinars, position papers, and resource links to inform and guide educators in developing and using their voice in education.

Assessment

http://serc.carleton.edu/NAGTWorkshops/assess/types.html

Though geared to the geoscience field, the list of assessment tools and their usage by the National Association of Geoscience Teachers provides information and examples that all teachers can apply in their classrooms.

Behavior Management

www.disciplinehelp.com

Master Teacher's "You Can Handle Them All" identifies 124 behaviors children may display at school or home, their causes and effects, and actions teachers and parents can take to help the child move beyond the behavior.

www.challengingbehavior.org/explore/pbs/process.htm

The Technical Assistance Center on Social Emotional Intervention for Young Children lists six steps essential to the process of positive behavior support.

Bullying

http://www.stopbullying.gov

Through this federal government site, teachers, parents, and students can access multiple resources for preventing and dealing with bullying and cyberbullying, including information on individual state's laws and policies.

www.stompoutbullying.org

Stomp Out Bullying™ is a national program that focuses on reducing and preventing bullying, cyberbullying, sexting, and other digital abuse. Its website offers an extensive list of resources to assist educators, parents, and teens.

Classroom Management

www.apa.org/education/k12/classroom-mgmt.aspx

The American Psychological Association offers in-depth information through classroom management teacher modules, including recommendations for the classroom, why they work, and an extensive FAQ list.

www.pecentral.org/climate/index.html

The PE Central site for physical education teachers devotes a large section to classroom management, with strategies and solutions any teacher can use.

English Language Learning

www.nabe.org

The National Association for Bilingual Education site represents bilingual education professionals and learners, offering resources, advocacy, and support for all languages and cultures.

www.ncela.gwu.edu

Resources at the official site of the National Clearinghouse for English Language Acquisition and Language Instruction Educational Programs include webinars, conferences, accessibility policies, and links to many related sites.

Forms and Templates

www.educationworld.com/tools_templates/index.shtml

Education World® lists a wide variety of downloadable templates, forms, and certificates on this section of its site.

Health and Safety

www.sshs.samhsa.gov/default.aspx

The Safe Schools/Healthy Students Initiative site provides information and links on grant-making programs for preventing violence and drug abuse, along with various resources.

www.webmd.com

WebMD® provides credible health information and tools for its management, with searches by symptoms and conditions, including ADHD and sleep disorders. For a look at the effects of sleep problems in children, see www.webmd.com/sleep-disorders/features/fixing-sleep-problems-may-improve-childs-grades-and-behavior.

International

www2.ed.gov/teachers/how/tech/international/index.html

The Teacher's Guide to International Collaboration provides materials to help teachers use the Internet to "reach out" globally.

Lesson Plans

www.free.ed.gov

Lesson materials for a wide array of subjects on this site are supplied by various federal agencies.

www.teachervision.fen.com

This site offers various resources to enhance curriculum, enrich students, and make teachers' professional lives a bit easier.

Parents

www.internet4classrooms.com/parents.htm

This resource guide is a good information source to share with your students' parents.

Professional Development

www.edweek.com

The online *Education Week* news resource covering current educational topics, issues, and events keeps you informed on the professional field.

www.nbpts.org

The National Board for Professional Teaching Standards site offers information on innovative teaching practices, standards, and being a highly effective teacher.

Students with Special Needs

www.LDOnline.org

This leading resource on learning differences provides extensive information about learning difficulties, including ADHD/ADD. Its extensive information is useful to teachers, parents, and students. ADHD-specific strategies are available at www.ldonline.org/article/Strategies_for_Teaching_Youth_with_ADD_and_ ADHD.

www.ncld.org

This National Center for Learning Disabilities site offers well-organized areas of resources, legislature updates, and information related to children and adults with learning differences.

www2.ed.gov/about/offices/list/osers/osep/index.html

The Office of Special Education Programs (OSEP), under the government division Office of Special Education and Rehabilitation Services, is a teacher and parent go-to source for all things official regarding special education.

Samples, Forms, and Checklists

In the next several pages, you will find examples and samples of items mentioned in alpha entries of this book. You may copy these pages for your use or download them from *ABC's Online*, www.kdp.org/teachingresources/ABConline.php. At *ABC's Online,* the website companion to this book, you also can access classroom tools, additional forms, and supplementary materials related to various alpha entries. Remember to check out the site as you design and manage your learning community.

Newsletter

Keep students' families informed and connected to class happenings and their child's world at school with regularly sent newsletters. Using a template keeps information consistent and speeds production time. Choose from these suggested newsletter columns to make your classroom newsletter reflect the needs and personality of your community. Also see **Newsletters**.

What's in a newsletter?

- Date of newsletter
- Contact info
- Word from the teacher
- Dates to Remember/Upcoming Events
- This Week We Study. This column lets parent know current units and lessons
- Things Our Classroom Needs. Keep your classroom stocked by sharing its needs in a regular column. List project needs, from paper towel tubes to volunteers, along with the dates items are needed
- Thank You to. . . . This column offers a note of appreciation to people who contributed to the classroom. List their names and contributions
- Congratulations to. . . . This column is a great place to recognize students for accomplishments outside school, such as an earned belt in karate or a Little League team win
- Reminders (timely homework guidelines, school policy, etc.)
- Fact of the Week
- Tips for Parents

Sample Newsletter

What's Happening

Ms. Janen's
Grade 3

Week or
Month Here

We're Studying

Language Arts: Metaphors   Math: Graphs
Science: States of matter   More: Map skills

LA bookmaking projects due next Thursday. Encourage creativity and polished work!

Look for daily math problems next week.

Work on 3 spelling words each night. Practicing builds confidence.

Spelling tip: Practice aloud and in writing. Spell in sand or salt as well as on paper.

Quizzes & Tests Tickler

This week's spelling test is postponed to Monday due to special assembly on Friday.

Students know to expect a "pop quiz" on multiplication this week. Get them calculating during dinner prep!

CONGRATULATIONS!

Josh Thompson and Caleb Fedders each scored goals in the finals soccer match, helping their team, The Tornados, win the game and season championship.

Good Luck!

Olivia Sager, JoJo Sams, and Alden Barrows head to Odyssey of the Mind regionals.

For the first time in Betsy Ross School history, a third grader (Danyelle Voss) has been chosen as Artist of the Month by the Art & Artisans Guild of Crandall County.

Things Our Classroom Needs

Do you have extra ribbon, lace, buttons, and scrap fabric, especially in earth tones? We are collecting for a special project.

The flu is going around again! Please send a small bottle of hand sanitizer to school with your child.

Upcoming Events

Third & Fourth Grade Family Night in 2 weeks! RSVP by phone or e-mail to Ms. Janen or return the form in your child's backpack.

Contact Ms. Janen
555.555.5655
Available M, T, & TH 10:45–11:15
I return messages within 24 hours.

Room Arrangements

Sample Classroom Arrangement 1

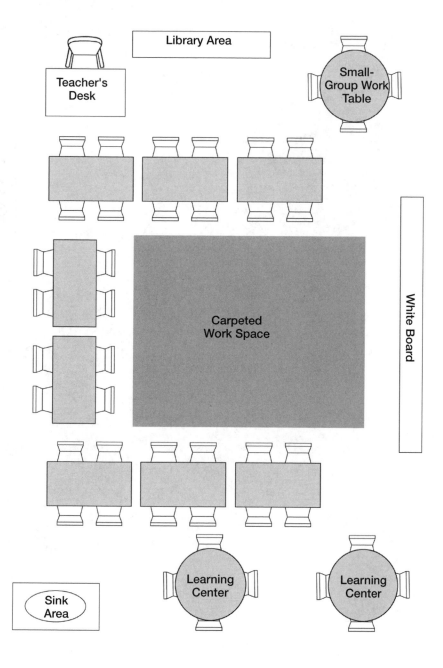

Sample Classroom Arrangement 2

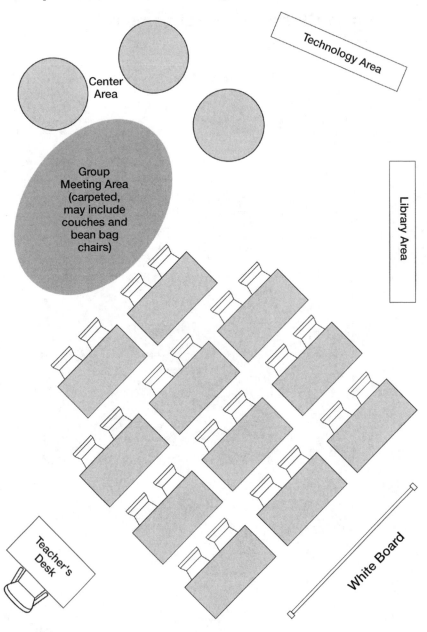

Checklists

Room Arrangement Checklist

As soon as you have access to the room in which you will teach, take an assessment and inventory of furniture, shelving, storage areas, and materials. If additional items are needed, check with the school and neighboring teachers for assistance before scouring family and friends' attics or shopping discount stores. Once you've assessed the classroom's physical needs, use this checklist to help you arrange the room for the best student flow and teacher viewpoints. Keep upcoming curriculum units and activities in mind. Consider these questions as you plan.

- Will students access learning centers?
- Do you want to make room for a quiet, comfortable place to read?
- Is technology available in your classroom?
- Taking into account activities you plan, how can you arrange the space to keep noise, disruptions, movement, and distractions at a minimum for you and the students?
- Is there easy access to materials, clean-up areas, sinks, outlets, and storage areas?
- Does your arrangement allow students to move from one area to another without disturbing others?
- What level of interaction would you like among students? Would you like to cluster students to encourage interaction or space apart desks to encourage independent work?
- What about you? How much work space do you need? Have you designated a personal storage area for yourself?
- Will you need a space for a classroom pet?
- Have you set aside a large area for group instruction and class meetings?
- Is the overall arrangement comfortable or cluttered?

Environment Checklist

Is your classroom student friendly and conducive to learning? Check it against this list and refer to **Environment** for additional information about "designing" your classroom atmosphere.

- The environment conveys a welcoming and comfortable atmosphere. ☐
- The environment suggests a sense of safety and security for students at the grade level being taught. ☐

- The room boasts a "chill–out corner," a get-away area decorated in soft, calming colors such as blue or green where students can relax. □
- Stimulating visual displays, manipulatives, and materials fill the room to galvanize students' curiosity about learning and current or upcoming curriculum content. □
- The classroom is orderly and organized. □
- Ample space separates classroom elements, such as desks, learning centers, and group areas, allowing students to move easily around the room. □
- The classroom provides space for each student to store personal belongings. □

Small classrooms or limited storage areas:
- Does the room look or feel cramped? □
- How can you add space? Students don't need to see everything all the time. Save space and keep students interested by displaying fewer materials more often. □
- Are you making the most of what is available? Would different storage containers be more effective or free up valuable space? See **Helping Tools** for a few ideas. □

Field Trip Checklist

Site check

Visit site prior to arranging field trip to determine:
- Time frame of trip □
- Lunch/snack facilities □
- Handicap accessibility □
- Appropriate chaperone ratio □
- Group/individual cost □
- Paperwork/administrative prep □
- Trip purpose defined (administrative request) with tentative agenda set □
- Field trip paperwork and permission submitted □
- Administration approval received □
- Transportation arranged □
- Permission slips and information letter written and sent home □

- Permission slips returned ☐
- Tickets/funding obtained ☐
- Trip prep ☐
- Chaperones identified ☐
- Chaperones trained ☐
- Students grouped with chaperones ☐
- Emergency information list compiled ☐
- Materials related to trip prepared ☐
- Site directions prepared ☐
- Student prep completed ☐

Parent-Teacher Conference Preparation Checklist

- Send a letter to parents inviting them to identify questions they would like you to address during the conference. (A proactive approach allows you to prepare) ☐
- Gather tests, anecdotal records, portfolios, and other work samples to show parents ☐
- Prepare an index card noting key items to cover at the conference. (See example that follows) ☐
- Arrange seating so that you and the parents are on the same level—at a large table or equal-sized chairs. Do not sit behind your desk. Set up an equal and welcoming arrangement ☐
- Dress and act professionally. Do not drink or smoke prior to the conference ☐
- Greet parents warmly. Be sure you know their proper names, especially in blended family situations ☐
- End the conference on a positive note and with a summary of the discussion and actions to be taken. Parents should leave with a sense of hope and encouragement for their child ☐

Parent-Teacher Conference Report

Parent-Teacher Conference Report

Student's Name _____ Date _____

Strengths

_____

_____

Concerns

_____

_____

Questions

_____

_____

Actions Recommended

_____

_____

_____

_____

_____

_____

_____

_____

Progress Report

Student Progress Report

Student _____ Grade _____

Teacher(s) _____ Date _____

Subject	Satisfactory Progress	Concerns to Address	Positive Developments
Reading			
Math			
Science			
Social Studies			
Language Arts			
Art			
Music			
Conduct			
Work Habits			

Photo Release Form

Parental/Legal Guardian Media Consent Form

I hereby consent to the use of any photographs or video tape taken of my child by the school or the local media for the purpose of advertising or publicizing events, activities, facilities, and programs of the _____ School in newspapers, newsletters, web pages, other publications, television, radio, and other communications and advertising media.

Please mark one of the choices below and return to school.

_____ Yes, I allow my child to be identified in any good news district or school publication.

_____ No, I do not want my child identified in any good news district or school publication.

PLEASE PRINT

Student's Name: _____

Address: _____

City: _____

State/Zip: _____

Signature: _____

Parent or Guardian Information:

Parent/Guardian's Name: _____

Address: _____

City: _____

State/Zip: _____

Signature: _____

Family Science Night

Promote family involvement with an event that features an aspect of the curriculum. One successful activity is Family Science Night. Invite students and their parents to the school for an evening of hands-on science activities. Although this event takes careful planning and detailed preparation, it is a wonderful opportunity for families to participate in their child's school, and it's an enjoyable learning experience for all who attend. Teachers who have conducted a successful Family Science Night used the following steps as a guide for the event. Good luck!

1. *Set a time and place.* Arrange a suitable date and select a room that can accommodate either several large tables or numerous small ones with enough space left for participants to engage in hands-on activities. Be sure to obtain permission and support for this event from your building administrator right away.

2. *Plan the activities.* Family Science Night activities need to be engaging and meaningful, yet simple enough for parents and children to accomplish in a short period of time. This evening is a good time to enlist volunteers. In fact, it's a must. Partner with preservice educators from a nearby university to plan, develop, and assist during the event. You also can seek assistance from upper grade or high school students and colleagues. Approach school clubs for help; members can count helping as a service activity.

3. *Obtain materials.* Determine what supplies you'll need, and seek funding or material donations from the school, parent-teacher organization, local businesses, or parents.

4. *Create directions.* Outline easy-to-follow steps for each activity and place copies at each table. The directions must be clear and concise so that students and parents can perform the experiments with minimal assistance from a teacher.

5. *Prepare invitations.* Create an invitation that includes an RSVP form so that you can plan accordingly. At this point, you know whether or not other classes are participating in the event. Ideally they are because working with a team of teachers divides the load of planning and running a curriculum night.

6. *Produce an activity pack.* Put together a list of all the activities available during the Family Science Night, along with directions, supplemental ideas, and resources for families to take home. Offering a take-home packet extends the benefit of the event beyond the one evening, giving families materials for trying experiments they didn't work on during Family Science Night,

along with additional activities. Having something to show for the evening's efforts is always a plus.

7. *Food and beverage.* Refreshments are welcoming and appreciated by attendees who didn't have time for dinner. However, providing them adds one more thing to your Do List and in your budget. Check with your school's parent-teacher organization for assistance with refreshments.

8. *Participation recognition.* Attendance ribbons or certificates of participation acknowledge and reward students and parents. They help validate the experience. One of these can go in the take-home packet.

9. *Organize.* With the help of a set-up committee, organize all materials and arrange the room ahead of time. Consider materials needed and activity requirements, such as access to water or an electrical outlet. Materials, activity centers, and presentations that give clear directions and look interesting and appealing encourage engagement.

10. *Greet.* Recruit volunteers to greet and register participants.

11. *Circulate.* Throughout the evening, go around the room to answer questions, address problems, and visit with your students and their families.

12. *Clean up.* By the end of the event, you will have had a very long day, so be sure you recruit a clean-up crew prior to the event. With the help of all your volunteers, you can leave the room as tidy as you found it.

13. *Share with the community.* Let the local media know about Family Science Night ahead of time in case a reporter or photographer can capture the event. If no one is available, send a brief article and several pictures for the paper's education section. Share the event's success with your school community too—through morning announcements, a newsletter, and the school's website. Promote good news about your school!

NEW TEACHER ADVOCATE

Your Partner For Success

YEAR 1

- Everything is new.
- Every day is busy.
- Every moment, waking and sleeping, is filled with *something* about teaching.

YOU WANT

- Quick tips
- Practical solutions
- Positive support
- Inspiration
- A breather (finally!)

YOU NEED

WHAT YOU GET

- Print, digital—or both
- Priced for members, nonmembers, and bulk subscriptions
- Four 16-page issues annually
- Filled with professional insights and classroom ideas
- Timely

Learn more and subscribe at kdp.org/publications/nta, or call 800.284.3167.

Teaching isn't a "lonely" profession . . .

. . . when you belong to a community of 45,000 other educators.

Learn more about Kappa Delta Pi, International Honor Society in Education, and its members who are committed to scholarship, service, leadership, and the pursuit of excellence.

kdp.org/aboutmembership

KAPPA DELTA PI
INTERNATIONAL HONOR SOCIETY IN EDUCATION

KAPPA DELTA PI • 3707 Woodview Trace • Indianapolis, IN 46268-1158 • 800-284-3167 • KDP.org